TIME
MOMAGEMENT

TIME MOMAGEMENT

How to get the time you need to do the things you want

A little book about goal setting, prioritizing, and managing your time during the challenging mama years

By: Marisa Volpe Lonic

ISBN-13: 9781071463802

Dedication

To my hubs for always supporting my crazy ideas.

To my kids for making me wiser, smarter, and way more efficient.

To my mom who did it all and paved my path.

To my haters for reminding me how important success is to me.

What moms are saying...

"A must read for any mom facing the daily struggles of balancing it all. Get ready to be inspired, motivated, and empowered in ways you didn't think possible."

-Mona, mom of 2

"Time Momagement is life changing. I never imagined a different way to live my hectic life as a working mom. Marisa outlines specific and efficient ways to make your time count for you."

-Gina, mom of 2

"You will find yourself laughing, crying, and saying "that's me"! Find the time to read this book; you will thank yourself in the morning!"

-Barbara, mom of 3

Contents

Foreword

How This Even Happened

I'm just a regular mom. Ok, well I'm not like a regular mom, I'm a cool mom. Wink. Hopefully you're also a fan of the movie *Mean Girls* and got that joke. Otherwise, I just started this book on a really bad note.

Back in 2016, I had just moved to a new city with my husband and two-year-old twins. I'd gotten a job promotion, and while I was slightly scared of what would happen to my work-life balance in a bigger role with a longer commute in a new city where I knew hardly anyone, I was never one to shy away from an opportunity, let alone a really awesome one. A few months into the gig, while I didn't have regret, I still had some unease about whether or not I was managing my time and my work-life balance well enough.

Here's the thing. I wanted to have a successful career. I also wanted to be an awesome mom—a mom who was present. And I wanted to be an appreciative and loving wife. And finally, I wanted to be myself, who liked to have manicured nails and enjoyed spending some time doing retail therapy now and then. Basically, I wanted it all. And I was determined to get it.

The truth was, I already had a lot of what I wanted, but I needed to fit it into the new normal. I needed it to fit into my life, to all our lives.

Week by week, I started making changes, doing things a bit differently, taking small steps that would eventually have a significant impact on me. Looking back now, I realize this challenge, this life event, this change, lit the match for me to become more efficient, more focused, and more capable of having it all—and then some. This wasn't the only time this happened, but it's the one I hold closest to my heart because it presented the biggest triggers to ignite those external (and internal) changes.

During that time, I was also working with a life coach in hopes of figuring out the magic recipe of how I was going to be able to achieve this balance and peace I so desperately wanted. The idea of starting a blog came up. I know, weird. How would a blog help me achieve my goals? Wasn't this just another thing to do? But, it was what I needed at the time. It was a creative outlet I could use to gather my thoughts, understand my needs, and inspire others.

I started writing regularly. I wrote about anything and everything: parenting, friendship, working, and everything in between. It was awesome, but I was totally directionless. I didn't want to be labeled as anything (not as a mom, a wife, an executive, a woman—nothing). I was petrified to let anyone read it. I wrote a blog about everything I was going through with no clear path of where I was headed—and I wrote as if I had an audience of thousands, even though the only person I allowed to read it was me.

Why? I wasn't ready.

Looking back and being barely older (I'm always young at heart) and slightly wiser, I realized, are we ever really ready? There's never a perfect time to do anything: have kids, move, start a blog, tell people about your blog. I'm a firm believer that it all happens for a reason though, so stay with me.

Fast forward a bit…just under two years to be exact.

At the start of every year, I write down the goals that I want to accomplish that year. On January 1, 2018, I wrote my list just like I had in previous years. On that list, I wrote: *Publish Blog.* It was weird. I wasn't really sure why I even wrote it. I hadn't touched the blog since I'd had my third baby the previous July. Bringing in a third kid had created a whole new layer of normalcy in my house, but only after it caused a lot of upheaval. It took about six months of exclusively pumping and getting sporadic sleep while still raising two other small humans to figure it all out before I could focus on other things. But, something told me to write it down anyway. To be honest, it was the first time I'd ever written a goal on that list without full intention of actually doing it.

When I wrote my list of annual goals, I was still fresh back at work from maternity leave. I could tell you a lot of flowery language about what the return to work was like, but I'll keep it simple. It fucking sucked.

It's not that I didn't like my job. I did.

It's not that I'd never gone back to work after maternity leave before. I had.

I felt something bigger this time though. I wanted to be more in control of my time, my schedule, and my energy. I wanted more.

I brainstormed a million ideas of a business I could start on my own that would afford me the flexibility and schedule I was yearning for. I had dabbled in photography. Should I do that? Should I become one of those "momtographers"? They seemed to be doing ok financially. Those newborn photoshoots are pricey! But, when I thought about it, it didn't do it for me. It didn't ignite or excite me. It didn't make me feel like I was tapping into my *real talents,* and as cliché as this is going to sound, *my true calling.*

Then, I thought about the blog that was still sitting there in the back of my mind. There was something to be said for it. Sure, it was kind of a hot mess. But isn't every mom kind of a hot mess, at least sometimes? I'd start there.

Ready or not, I did it. In May 2018, I published the blog and finally shouted it out from the social media rooftops. If you want to know what vulnerability feels like, write about yourself and then ask everyone on the internet to read it. It's ridiculously uncomfortable, yet an incredible sense of accomplishment all mingled into one intense start-up experience.

I wrote regularly for the next several months. I better defined my story of managing the life of a mom, a working mom specifically, since that was the life I was living. I didn't feel like an expert in anything. I just wanted to share my stories, and what had worked for me in hopes it would help other moms and give a voice to a well deserving community. Women I'd never met started emailing me telling me how much they loved my stories and appreciated my advice. Acquaintances from high school DM'ed me how grateful they were for my posts. My following grew, and I started making a small dent in the impact I'd intended to create. I still wasn't quite sure of my expertise, but I knew I was helping, and that's what mattered most.

Then it happened.

My niche.

My forte.

My calling.

I figured out the area I needed to build and focus on. I'd already been doing it to a degree, but now, I was going to give it a name, a pedestal, and some real attention.

People would ask me constantly, "How do you find the time…to have a blog, to work full-time, to parent three kids, etc. etc. etc.?" After hearing this question repeatedly, something finally clicked. I knew what I had to focus on, what would help moms the most: time. Getting back the time they'd lost when they became moms; being able to structure their days so that at the end they felt empowered and not defeated; helping them set attainable goals and offering tangible steps on how to get there. I needed to share this specific message because if I can do what I'm doing, you can do what you want to do too. And so, it all clicked together. I became a *time momager*.

I'd always been a self-starter, a planner, and very goal oriented. These skillsets amplified my abilities to not only have it all, but to be at peace, be happy, and be able to achieve a lot during the busy, challenging, and chaotic time of having young kids. I'm no time goddess. I can't perform time miracles. And I'm also not a total time management weirdo who sticks to her calendar 100% of the time. I just figured out some shit that works, and I want to help my people out. And you, moms, are my people.

When I thought of the title for this book, Time Momagement, I was in the shower. I don't know about you, but that is often where I get my best ideas. Maybe it's the hot water? Maybe it's the quietness? Maybe it's the me-time? Sad, but true—you moms know a hot shower that's longer than 10 minutes feels like a visit to the spa. Anyway, I thought of it and immediately wrote it down when I got out, because, well-mom brain. I didn't want to forget it! I thought about this word a lot and how much sense it makes for the concept of managing your time to be a mom's forte and not a man's. Sorry, men. I only bring you into this because I swapped 'mom' for 'man' in the word as you probably already figured out. Not because I'm a man-hater. I'm not. I married one and am raising three. Back to that title though, women, and moms especially, are so damn good at managing things, aren't we? We take care of everyone, everything, and every other person or thing in between. We keep households running, children thriving, significant others satisfied, careers growing, friendships going, and ourselves alive, often making it all look easy.

By the way, notice how I said *ourselves alive* back there? That's totally on purpose. I bet sometimes you feel that's all you do for yourself. You're the last person you think about when it comes to priorities. You're the last thing to take care of on your to-do list. You're the, "I'll start that tomorrow" or "I'll get to that later." And we all know what happens to that last thing on your list, the least of your priorities. It rarely gets done. That's about to change, mama.

I used to do this all the time. I used to find any excuse to not do something for myself:

It's too expensive.

It's unnecessary.

It's not worth it.

It's too indulgent.

I'll do it tomorrow.

I'll do it later.

I'll do it when I get to it.

I don't deserve it.

Etc. Etcetera. ETCETERA!

Trust me, I've said it, felt it, and basically could write a book on it. Which I did, you're reading it! So, listen up. I've been there with you, feeling like you can barely come up for air with every single thing you're doing for every single person in your life. It doesn't feel good. And for me it usually led to something like this:

A build of resentment, which leads to some passive aggressive or short circuit behavior, which then portrays itself as a somewhat psychotic woman who is crying about wanting to feel normal again leading to a slight mental breakdown, followed by a manicure-pedicure and short-lived period of time before the vicious cycle would repeat itself.

Have you been there? Are you there now? If so, read on.

I had to break the cycle and figure out what it would take for me to feel, most days, like I had it together in all areas of my life, including caring for myself. I knew when I deposited all my time into everyone else's bank account, I was broke, in all senses of the word. I also knew I was a ridiculously strong woman, who had never let the words, "I can't do it" be her reality.

Beyoncé says it best in her hit song *Run the World (Girls)*. If you don't know the lyrics to that jam, go look them up stat.

Basically, as women, as moms, we know how to get shit done.

And we're about to set sail and start learning and implementing some of those awesome time management skills we have (or are about to get in this book) and, most importantly, ensure we include the captain of the ship in the time plan, ourselves.

Before we dive in, here are a few key pointers that will help you get the most out of this book:

- **Get in the zone.** If you can read this book during a quiet time, when you're not distracted by a hundred other things, like your kids, your husband, your work, your email, your favorite (or not favorite) TV show, I recommend that. For me, this time is the evening once everyone is all tucked into bed. If you're a morning person, maybe do it then—during those silent hours of the wee morning before anyone is awake and starting to ask for milk or cereal or butt wiping? What about a lunch hour at work? Your commute? Naptime? I want you to be able to focus and invest in this time for *yourself.* So, pick a time, *any time*, that makes sense with your life and gives you the opportunity to focus.

- **Be ready to work it.** Remember, dreams don't work unless you do. So, don't look at this as another thing to do. Look at it as a step toward achieving your dreams. I think we can all admit, with a little more time and sanity, we could, would, and will accomplish some great things. Hell, even if it is something simple like putting on make-up every day. It's your life and your time, so be ready to take some steps, own the work, and receive the sweet reward you're hoping for afterward.

- **Trust the process.** Every time I've felt like I've hit a brick wall in my life where I wasn't going in the exact direction I was hoping for, or I wasn't, *God forbid,* totally in control of the exact next step, I've taken a deep breath and reminded myself to *trust the process.* Even if that process seems unnecessary or impractical, or not meant for you, just do it, read it, think about it, and let it happen. Trust me, and trust the process, baby.

This thing about time and managing it is that it's really more about momaging it. Time momagement is about handling the impossible, clarifying the important, prioritizing the necessary, and still feeling like you love yourself and your life at the end of each day. So, let's start momaging.

Chapter 1

Do It for Them and Do It for You

"Your influence as a mother is powerful. Don't waste it. Little eyes are watching you."
                                    -Unknown

In this chapter you'll learn:

- How to combat mom guilt and give yourself permission to care for yourself.
- The difference between worthiness and entitlement.
- Why saying yes more often may be the answer to your problem.

Mom guilt. It's a real thing. You've felt it. You feel it. Often.

Mom guilt doesn't discriminate either. It hits up all moms. Working moms, stay at home moms, helicopter moms, laid-back moms, millennial moms, married moms, single moms, *all the moms.*

So, if you're feeling any ounce of mom guilt right now, for even wanting to change your time momagement ways; if you're feeling a drop of mom guilt for wanting to prioritize yourself back into your life; if you're feeling a millimeter of mom guilt for reading this book right now instead of doing something else for someone else, come on-you know what I'm talking about. I'm sure the list goes something like this:

Cleaning up the dinner dishes

Packing tomorrow's lunches

Folding the four loads of laundry you washed today (or yesterday-no judgement)

Checking your emails

Stop.

Stop right now.

Because I'm here to tell you this crucial fact—you're not only doing this for *you*. That's right. Being a better time momager and prioritizing things *you* want to do into your day, your week, your life is also for *them*, those tiny humans who depend on you so much. So, if for a second you're questioning whether the act of time momagement is a selfish one, I'm going to be the one who gives you a visual or audio (however you're reading or listening to this) smack across the face and tells you to cut that shit out, mama.

A few years ago, a friend of mine sent me an evite to go to Napa for the day with a bunch of other women, all of them moms. It was cleverly called *Moms' Day Away*. I know what you're thinking. What's not to love about everything I've described thus far? Wine, women, Napa Valley...sounds like a dream, doesn't it? As amazing as this day sounded to me, I didn't jump the gun at going. In fact, I was embarrassingly called out when I didn't RSVP by the due date. This wasn't entirely on accident. I was busy, and it had definitely slipped my mind, but I also hadn't convinced myself I *should* go. I had a laundry list of excuses why I shouldn't, many of them with the common denominator of guilt. Let me explain.

I shouldn't go because I'm a working mom and spending an entire day away from my kids on the weekend isn't right. I barely see them as it is.

I shouldn't go because I have to do laundry, grocery shop, meal plan, cook, <u>fill in the blank</u> with any and every other thing I typically do on the weekends.

I shouldn't go because $140 is a lot of money to spend on myself and I'll have nothing to show for it in the end.

Do you know what all these things have in common?

One word. Worthiness.

I shouldn't go because I'm not worthy.

You could swap this phrase out with all of the excuses mentioned above, and it would still lead you to the same, exact destination: Worthyville, USA.

Despite my internal worthiness battle and lots of arguments with my favorite person to fight with: myself, I did end up going. This day taught me so, so much (and by the way, was also so, so fun). When it was all over, I returned home feeling refreshed and grateful I'd decided to go. But still, being the analytical thinker I am, I reflected a lot about this decision, this experience, and this saga many moms face daily.

The worthiness saga.

This wasn't the first time I'd felt this inner struggle, and it certainly wouldn't be the last, but I was going to start looking at it with a different set of lenses: the "I'm worth it" lenses. And what changed everything for me were the most important people I know: my kids.

When I thought about the fact that feeling unworthy was something I was doing, an example I was setting for them, a potential trait they would inherit and perhaps even exercise in their own lives, I said, *"Hellll no, mother-eff'er."* I didn't want my kids to *ever* feel like they *shouldn't* do something for any of those unworthy reasons. I wanted them to try new things. I wanted nothing to stop them from doing what they wanted to do, especially some ridiculous, unwarranted inner lack of worthiness. I realized I had to step up and *be* worthy so I could *raise* worthy kids, kids who knew they deserved to be happy, who treated themselves with respect, and who took good care of the most important people to me: them.

Now, I may be a lot of things, but one thing I'm not is a liar. So, I won't sit here and tell you I don't still battle the mom guilt beast sometimes. I most certainly do. I don't think I'll ever be able to totally rid that bitch from my life. She's been here since the moment I found out I was expecting, and I'll bet she's here to stay. But, I've set some clear boundaries to ensure she only visits sparingly. She and I are in a much better place now, one I feel extremely *worthy* of being in.

When you start to look at taking care of yourself as also taking care of your kids, you inevitably start to feel less guilty about it. As moms, we live for our kids, so why wouldn't self-care qualify as one of the many selfless tasks we're doing for them?

Worthiness...Don't Get it Twisted with Entitlement

Because it most certainly is not.

If there's anything that really bothers me, it's entitlement. I'm sure you've come across an entitled person in your life at some point or another. I like to call them assholes. You know who I'm talking about.

The colleague who is too good to put in the work

The mom who refuses to accept the fact that her kid did anything wrong

And probably her kid, who is a total spoiled brat

Entitlement is the most unattractive, obnoxious, and ugly trait you can have in my book. Coming from someone who has worked her ass off to get to where she is, I know firsthand the value of a dollar *and* an opportunity. I do my best to take nothing for granted and I try my damnedest to be grateful every single day. Don't you act entitled around me, honey. I see right through it, and it will get you nowhere in my friendzone.

But, don't get your entitlement definition twisted. Entitlement is *shit* and worthiness is *the shit*, even though some people get *that shit* confused.

Here's how entitlement is different than worthiness:

Entitlement	Worthiness
I deserve this—it should happen.	I'm so glad it is happening.
Thanks, I deserve this.	Thanks, I'm so appreciative.
You owe me.	I owe me.
I'm better than you.	I'm awesome, and so are you.

Entitled people expect a lot, and when they don't receive it, they're pissed off and miserable. Nothing is ever enough. They feel like the world owes them something. They attract negativity because deep down, even if they don't appear negative superficially, they absolutely are. These are *not* the peeps you should be getting close with if you want to be the best time momager you can be. You may not be able to rid them entirely from your life, but you can and most certainly should keep a healthy distance.

Worthy people expect a lot, and when they don't receive it they either accept it or figure out a way to make it happen. They're satisfied, yet proactive, determined, and relentless. When they feel like the universe isn't delivering, they knock again, ask politely, and perhaps even offer something to barter in return. These are the peeps you should be gravitating to and emulating. These are the ones who are going to make you live your best and most worthy life, mama.

As I said, entitlement is just about *the worst* quality you can have in my book. Consequently, I, myself, am hyper aware and sometimes almost too 'self-questioning' about whether or not my behavior is coming across as worthy or entitled. I've found that when I start to think about this too much, I usually eff up a really good thing. I'm not perfect, far from it, so I'll give you a prime example of how my inner-self talked me into believing I didn't deserve a seat at the table one day, a feeling I'm sure many of you have felt before, in your career or your social group.

My boss had a planned vacation and wasn't able to attend a conference that other company heads would be attending. She asked me to go in her place. I was excited for the opportunity to be able to attend this event, network with peers in the industry, and learn a ton from the presenters of the organization sponsoring it. The event was followed by a happy hour that everyone was invited to and then a dinner that only a select few were invited to. I'd been extended an invite to both. Yet for some reason, I had a slight inner dialogue on whether or not the dinner was a pity invite or not. Yes, I had convinced myself that

I was being invited to that dinner because of obligation and not the importance of my being there.

These feelings and doubts only grew throughout the day as I sat in a room with older and pretty arrogant individuals who didn't know me. They asked who I was and why my boss wasn't at the event. I felt like I had to prove myself all day long. I made sure I asked intelligent questions. I purposefully raised my hand to comment on areas where I could add value. I worked my ass off that day to not only learn a bunch of *new shit* but also show everyone around me I knew *my shit*. I'd been in the industry for over seven years. I could certainly hold my own at the table. I leaned in, hard, but also in a very gracious and self-conscious sort of way.

When we went to the happy hour, I nervously mingled and tried to figure out who was attending the dinner and who wasn't. If there's anything I never want to portray, it's entitlement, and if there's any feeling I'd like to avoid, it's the embarrassing one where I feel like I'm not worthy of being somewhere. And that day, I felt that way, hardcore.

By the time the president of our company started wrapping up the happy hour so the non-invited dinner guests would leave and the invited ones would stick around to head over to the restaurant, I had convinced myself my invite was a mistake, and I needed to figure out a way to *not* go to the dinner. I didn't want to look like an entitled attendee or an embarrassed pitiful attendee—both of whom shouldn't actually be there. I walked over to her and made one of the biggest mistakes I've ever made in my career. I self-sabotaged my invitation, my presence, my worthiness.

"Meg," I said. "You don't need me to be at that dinner, do you?" She was taken aback and, of course, so was I. What the hell had I just said and done? What was I even thinking? My internal worthiness battle had just beat the shit out of my intelligent mind and won. The president of our company now thought I was a total asshole who didn't *want* to attend this incredibly important and prestigious dinner that she, herself, had organized. I couldn't have done worse. I mean, if I had left without saying anything and pretended I just didn't get the invite, I think I would have left a better impression that day.

"Oh," she reacted. "Well, if you need to head home, feel free. It's ok." I politely argued, "Oh no, of course I can go to the dinner. I just didn't know if you felt it was necessary."

Foot in mouth again. I couldn't fix it. It was done, and I was leaving the happy hour, my career advancement, my reputation of being an ambitious, hard-working, committed, and bright employee at the door.

I headed toward the metro station and contemplated what I'd just done. I couldn't believe I'd thought so hard about this stupid invitation and that I'd convinced myself I wasn't worthy of actually going. What a disaster. The only proud moment I had that evening was the fact that I didn't pity myself all night. I got home at a reasonable hour and went to get some ice cream with my family. I knew I was definitely worthy of doing that.

Fighting the worthiness battle is something I still do sometimes, but the more aware I've become of just how different worthiness and entitlement are and how deep down I know I'm far from the latter, the more at peace I am with feeling worthy. Will I still walk into a board room, or school pick up, or even a clothing store sometimes and feel totally out of my comfort zone because I think everyone else is smarter, in better shape, or more put-together than me? Yes, I absolutely will. But, in exercising my worthiness muscle over the years, I've gotten much stronger and more self-aware to know I belong there just as much as everyone else.

Balancing the Yes and No

Most moms fall into this similar trap: saying yes too often to others and no too frequently to themselves.

Can you bake something for the PTA fundraiser? Yes!

Can you make me a sandwich? Yes!

Can you drive me to Bobby's house? Yes!

Can Bobby come over? Yes!

Can we host the Smiths for dinner this weekend? Yes!

Can we host Thanksgiving? Yes!

Can you volunteer in the kindergarten classroom? Yes!

Can you complete this report by Friday? Yes!

Can you do four loads of laundry every other day of the week? Yes!

But, what about these?

Can you read this awesome book? Not sure, I am usually exhausted by the time I sit down to read.

Can you get away for a few days with the girls? Probably not.

Can you get away for a night out with the girls? Maybe (but then you bail).

Can you do nothing for no one for an hour today? Definitely not.

Can you spend 30 minutes a day exercising or doing something healthy for yourself? I don't have 30 minutes a day to spend on myself.

Not every moms' night out or girls' trip or opportunity in your career or even hour at the gym is going to be something you take yourself up on. It's a balancing act. But, I imagine your problem probably isn't saying yes to too many things for you right now. It's likely saying no to too many of those things. You're off balance with momaging everyone else's time and not momaging yourself into that schedule. So, begin here. Give yourself permission to let the guilt go...to your hater's house...and let it stay awhile.

Next time you're faced with an opportunity to do something for you, ask yourself this question:

How will I feel after this?

Working backward is usually a good way to give yourself an honest answer if you should make it happen and if you should momage it into your time.

How will I feel after my work out?

How will I feel if I spend the next 30 minutes reading?

How will I feel tomorrow if I go out with the girls tonight?

The answer to the last one might be hungover, but it might also be connected, rejuvenated, or less stressed. Think about the end result and base your decision on that. This will hopefully turn some of your current excuses and ultimate 'no's' into 'yes's.'

Let's Recap

- Remember, it's not all about you. Being a time momager and prioritizing yourself sets the example of worthiness for your kids. You taking care of you shows them how to take care of them.
- Don't let your laundry list of excuses convince you not to do something. Know it's just worthiness masking itself in different costumes. Undress it. A naked unworthiness is much easier to combat than one in a fancy suit.
- Know the difference between worthiness and entitlement. Practice worthiness. Ditch entitlement.
- Work backward. When you're volleying between saying no or yes to an opportunity or activity, ask yourself how you'll feel after the act is done. Let that be a determining factor in helping you decide whether or not you want to invest in it.

Chapter 2

Get Your Shit Together

"It's not about having the time. It's about making the time."
-Unknown

In this chapter, you'll learn:

- Ways to gain clarity on your time momagement goals.
- To identify actionable steps you can take *right now* to get there.
- How to organize your time and find areas where you might be wasting it.
- When you should multitask…and when you shouldn't.

One of the most important things you can do to create more balance, less stress, and overall happiness in your life is to get organized, or as I named this chapter: get your shit together. When your house, your family, your work, or your mind are not in order, neither are you. These things all correlate. Think about how you feel after you organize your closet or purge old toys that have been cluttering up, or perhaps even dominating, every part of your home and then drop off a huge donation bag to the Goodwill. You feel lighter. You feel cleaner. You feel like you actually have space in your house (and in your brain) for things that matter more. Sometimes, it's nice not to refill that space once you declutter it. The minimalism is so beautiful and fresh and looks like a gorgeous page out of an IKEA catalog. Clean lines, no clutter, beautiful blonde Swedish minimalism.

But how do you get your shit together when you have a lot of shit to handle? And I know, you have a lot of shit to handle, because I do too. Your house, your kids, your work, your husband or partner, your PTA fundraiser, your volunteering duties. It can be, dare I say, overwhelming? Where do you start? Is your house more important than your work? Are your kids more important than your significant other? Which kid comes first? How do you even start prioritizing what you need to do? I hope these questions are not stressing you out and making you want to close this book, curl up in the fetal position and turn on some mindless reality TV right now. Hell no, girlfriend! You bought this book because you're ready to make things happen. You're ready to get your shit together. You're ready to momage your time *right now.*

So, let's do it, mama. Let's start this very minute. I'm all about an organized life, and the first part of being able to momage your time is to know how you want to spend that time. What is important to you? If time (or lack thereof) weren't an excuse, how would you spend it? Basically, what are some time momagement goals you want to achieve?

Here are some examples I often hear:

I want to exercise more.

I want to spend more time with my kids, with my husband, with my friends, or even with myself.

I want to work less.

I want to get a massage or go to the spa.

I want to change jobs.

I want to move or buy a house.

I want to start a business.

Here's where getting your shit together makes sense. If you don't know how you want to spend your time, you will end up wasting it away! You need to know exactly what you want to do (or not do) in order to fully reap the benefits of the work you're about to do.

Let me give you an example:

Kara has two kids under the age of four. She works full time, and while she enjoys her job, she's constantly struggling with juggling all the moving parts of being a working mom. By the time she gets home from the office, she's too exhausted to cook dinner and ends up feeding her kids something unhealthy before she's racing to give them baths and get them to sleep. Then, she and her husband usually watch a show together while eating take-out. By 9 p.m. she's falling asleep on the couch but still needs to pack diaper bags, clean up the kitchen, and get ready for the next day. Kara constantly feels like she spends no time on herself and wishes she could feel less guilty about the parenting choices she's making, particularly about those unhealthy dinners.

Does Kara sound like you? If so, please don't take this the wrong way, but Kara needs to get her shit together. It's not that she's doing it all wrong. She's not. It's that she doesn't have clear, specific time momagement goals, so she doesn't know how to fathom the idea of fitting any of it into her busy life and schedule. Makes sense, right?

Without clarity, how can you really know what you want…or what you don't?

The first thing you (and Kara) need to do is get some of that clarity. So, stop right now. Stop reading and start making a list. Get a pen and start brainstorming. If you had all the time in the world, what would you do with it? What would make you feel less stressed? Less unhappy? Less overwhelmed? Less resentful? More fulfilled? More engaged? More balanced? Write down whatever comes to mind. We're going to narrow this list down in a minute, so don't worry about overdoing it.

Your time momagement goals are going to give you the clarity you need to get organized and start turning your time fantasies into time realities. Like I said, if you don't know how you want to spend your time, you will end up wasting it away and feeling like you don't have any time—which is probably how you already feel in your life right now.

How You Actually Spend Your Time vs. How You Want to Spend Your Time

Here's what I'm talking about. These are the things you are probably already doing and also things that are eating up your precious, precious time. These are the things that are preventing you from doing all of the other things that you wish you had time for. And these are the things that are also *extremely easy* to change in order to make time for the things you *actually want*, the things that are going to make you feel more productive, more accomplished, more satisfied, more fulfilled and more balanced. I promise you.

Time Spent on Social Media

Did you know the average person spends the equivalent of five years of their life on social media?[1]

In fact, according to an article in the NY Post, the average American person also checks their phone 80 times per day.[2]

---

[1] Statistic from www.socialmediatoday.com

[2] "Americans check their phones 80 times a day: a study," NY Post, November 8, 2016, https://nypost.com/2017/11/08/americans-check-their-phones-80-times-a-day-study/

Besides the fact that this is a *huge* time suck, it's also super unhealthy, and I don't mean only the blue light rays for your eyes. I mean for your soul. Don't even pretend when you're checking your social media you're not comparing yourself to everyone and everything on there.

How is she so skinny after birthing a child ten days ago?

How does she not look like a hot mess with four kids under six?

Why is her husband the most awesome man alive?

How is it even humanly possible for their house to be that clean?

Let me give you a quick sidebar reality check here, mama.

People's *social media lives* are not their *real lives*. So, stop going down the social media rabbit hole and feeling bad for yourself. Nobody likes a pity party. Put on your positive pants, crank up some gangsta rap, and remember, it just ain't real.

I'm not telling you to delete your social media and make some drastic change. I have social media and I'm not about to be a hypocrite. Like I said before, I'm no liar. If you want to delete it though, please, go ahead. I'm not going to stop you. One of my besties did this for a summer and told me she automatically felt lighter and happier—two things I know I enjoy. I *will* tell you, though, to start limiting. Give yourself less time per day to indulge in this time suck. How long is *really* *necessary* per day to get your social fix? Five minutes? Ten minutes? Twenty minutes? Set a timer on your phone and once it goes off, stop. There are even apps that time the amount of time you spend on your phone. Personally, I haven't found one that works for me because I am on my phone a lot, but I'm actually doing things I want to do on there, like listening to awesome audiobooks or podcasts, organizing my calendar or to-do lists, or prepping my marketing and social media posts. All things I do on my commute, by the way.

Another quick fix is to turn off your social media notifications. You don't need to check your likes or comments instantaneously. By the way, don't we all know we have to play it cool on social media anyway? I mean you can't like a comment as soon as it appears? You don't want to appear as though you're glued to your phone, do you?

Schedule your limited social media time and get ready for so much more time for all the things you want, not this time sucking, ego punching, interruptive activity.

Time Spent Watching Terrible TV

Girlfriend, I'm right there with you on the Real Housewives of Everywhere. It's an addictive drug that I used to dabble in and occasionally still do. So, no judgement if you're a Real Housewives fan.

I'm not saying I never watch TV. I do. But I don't watch it every day. And I don't have cable. Yeah. It's true. I'm sure you're in quite a bit of shock right now and maybe even finding me slightly less relatable due to this drastic step I've decided to take in my life. Let me tell you a little more about this before you write me off. I have many more pages of good shit I need you to read instead of the bullshit you'll likely be reading if you put this book down and pick up your phone. So, listen up, mama. I'm going to tell you the story of why I don't have cable anymore.

Prior to having my third son and shortly before starting maternity leave, my hubs and I consciously decided to get rid of cable. We had hit the point in our contract where the good deal promo was coming to an end, and our prices had been jacked up, even after I had made the famous 'threatening to cancel our service phone call,' which, by the way, had always worked in the past. So, we thought to ourselves, "Let's try a cableless life."

Before you start placing me in a weird category of someone who doesn't watch TV, I need you to understand that I'm still a normal human. I dress cool (at least I think so). I balayage my hair. I know a fair amount of what's happening in pop culture. I live near a major city. I listen to everything from 90s hip-hop to inspirational podcasts (both are an education). Basically, I'm pretty well-rounded and I'm not living in a bubble here.

When I went cable-free, it was a pretty risky time to do it. I mean, when you are gearing up for multiple night feedings and a lot of alone time with your baby, TV can become your temporary bestie. I thought to myself if I could survive without cable during maternity leave, I could survive without cable altogether. And I did.

What a cableless life has actually given me is:

a. A lot more time
b. Less bullshit taking up space in my head
c. A closer relationship with my spouse

d. And, I like to think, smarter brain cells

Like you, I have my own real-life drama, stress, and icky stuff I can't avoid in my life. When I stopped watching everyone else's on reality TV, I felt so much cleaner. I still have Netflix and Amazon Prime (I mean if you don't have Amazon Prime as a mom something is seriously wrong with you), but when you have to make a conscious decision to choose something to watch rather than just flipping to a channel and letting Bravo determine what you're watching (and commercials taking up a third of that time), you tend to make better decisions. You also tend to watch less TV, unless you get caught in a binge sesh. But, I know if you're reading this book, you're not going to let that happen, because you've got other things you want to do with that time. Am I right, mama? Don't answer that yet, you're only on chapter two. But really, who cares if Lisa Vanderpump and Kyle Richards had another fight or if Shannon Beador's divorce was finalized? I told you I was a fan.

So, stop watching or just start limiting your time-wasting shows. Trust me, it's going to lift you up and put you on a-whole-nother level in your time momagement game. Like I said, I don't totally disconnect. I allow myself a Real Housewife indulgence now and then, typically it's when I'm traveling for work, which is only a few times per year. I'll treat myself to some room service and lounge in a king-sized bed wearing that softer than a baby's bottom robe and letting Bravo rule my life for a few hours. Everyone's got to have these moments sometimes.

Time Spent Complaining or Shit Talking

Who doesn't love a little rant? I mean every now and then, we all need to vent. But when this starts becoming how you regularly spend your time, mama, you've got a problem.

Negative talk is like a cancer. It grows and can become uncontrollable. It starts taking over your life and pushing down anything remotely positive. It attracts the wrong type of people to be in your circle. Before you know it, you've been nixed from anything and everything with real value in your life because you're now known as the Negative Nancy or the Debbie Downer of your group.

I know I like to be surrounded by people who lift me up, not ones who bring me down, and I know you probably do too. So, next time you're about to call up your friend and start a good gossip fest or walk over to the water cooler when you-know-who is standing there, rethink it. You'll never get those 20 minutes back, and I'm sure you can think of so many other things you'd rather be doing during that time.

Your Time Momagement Goals

Are you still unsure of how you want to fill in your non-existent time gaps? Maybe you've even thought of a few more since you started your list. Take a few minutes right now to pull out a pen and paper, your phone, or anything else where you can jot down information. Personally, I think a journal works best for this type of work, and I love me a pretty little notebook. If a receipt and a half-eaten crayon are all you have right now, that works too. Don't fret. Just do it.

Make your official list: the "My Time Momagement Goals" list. Put anything and everything that comes to mind on it. You're brainstorming after all. No idea is too farfetched. Do you want to go to Italy? Write it down. Do you want to lose weight? Write it down. Do you just want to sleep eight hours, in a row? Write. It. Down. Write it all down, mama. Go ahead. I'll wait.

Still waiting.

I'll be waiting for a while.

Until you're done.

So, make your list.

And make it count.

Now that you've got your list of ways you want to spend your time, circle one way you want to spend your time on a daily basis, one way you want to spend it on a weekly basis and finally one way you want to spend it on an annual basis. Some examples of these might be:

Daily: I want to work out for 30 minutes per day.

Weekly: I want to spend an hour with my kid one on one per week.

Annually: I want to take a family vacation to Hawaii this year.

By the way, did you notice how freakin' specific the above-mentioned examples are? They're clear, unarguable ways to spend your time. You can't argue if you worked out today for 30 minutes. Either you did, or you didn't. Thirty minutes is 30 minutes.

Take a look at your three circled time actions. Are they specific enough? Are they clear-cut, black and white, indisputable actions? Is there any hue of gray in there? If so, re-word.

For example:

I want to lose weight (gray, so very gray).

I want to lose 5 pounds this month (as black as my favorite mascara).

Do this now.

Once again, I'll be here waiting.

Do this with so much intention, because it's one of the most important steps of this whole damn process.

If you're feeling stuck, ask yourself how you'd measure that time momagement goal. For example, if you wrote down, "Eat healthier" and circled this for your daily time momagement goal, ask yourself, "How will I measure this?" Does it mean eating more vegetables? Does it mean eating fewer desserts or fried foods? Does it mean meal prepping? Does it mean cooking at home vs. going out to eat? These questions all point toward a measurable target. Without a measurable target, you won't know for sure if you're succeeding and you'll be more likely to slip and fall when you're walking in your time momagement stilettos.

Ok, you've got your time momagement goals. Now, time, where you at? At this point, you're probably looking at your list and thinking, "Awesome, but how do I find the time to actually do these things?" Am I right or am I right?

You may still be skeptical, and you may not be sold yet on this idea of getting all this time to do all this amazing stuff you've brainstormed. But, I promise you, you *do* have the time because you're about to *make* the time. That's right! Put on your apron, Suzie Q, and get out your rolling pin. You are going to bake up some delicious, low-carb, low-cal time. I bet you can almost smell it cooking right now.

Pause. WTF am I even talking about?

Everyone has the same 24 hours in the day, yet some people do a lot more in those 24 hours than others. As moms, we do a lot. There's no denying that. Let's be honest. We are super-fucking-human. Yet, if you're face to face or in front of a mirror with that powerful, dominating, subhuman and ask, "What have you done for you lately?" (to the tune of Janet Jackson's eighties hit song of course), she would likely answer, "Oooh oooh yeah. Nothing." Sad, but true. And if you asked her why, she'd likely say, the four words most of us moms say every damn day: "I don't have time."

Mama, I'm about to give you a cold, hard, slightly harsh dose of my time momagement reality. I hope you still like me after I say it. One time, when I said this at a seminar I was leading, I

27

heard someone whisper under her breath, "You suck." So, whatever not-so-nice thing you feel like saying to me as you read this book right now, I want you to know, I don't take it personally because I know sometimes real love is tough love, and I'm about to give you some of that true love right now.

Listen up. It's not that you don't *have* time. It's that you're not *making* the time. Sorry, not sorry. I know your life is busy. I know your life is complicated. I know you have 101 responsibilities. I also know you want to figure out a way to prioritize yourself and your goals along with these responsibilities. And that's why you're reading this book. So, don't worry, you're about to learn how to make that time, badass mama style.

Making the Time

So, here we go. In my best Julia Child voice, "Making time is actually not that hard. And it requires just three easy steps."

Step 1

Take out your calendar. I use my third arm, or my phone, as my calendar mainly because it's super convenient. It reminds me automatically 15 or 30 minutes before the event, and it's basically attached to me most of the time, so that is what works best for me. I lean on my phone calendar like my kids lean on me. All. The. Time. I will say, when I want a more holistic view, I like to view my calendar on my laptop (which syncs up with what displays on my phone of course), so I can see a month or week out without squinting and having to wear my old lady reading glasses. If you prefer an old school paper calendar hanging on your fridge or in your office, go for it. Whatever works. What you need to remember though, is your calendar should be treated with the utmost level of respect since she is going to be your right hand in this process. She will be your accountability when you feel like bailing and your brain when you will likely forget things because we all know mom brain is a real thing. So, find the best device or printed version that works for you and befriend her, mama.

Step 2

Schedule that shit in. If your daily goal is spending 20 minutes of uninterrupted time reading with your kids, put it in there. Think about the time of day that would make the most sense. Choosing a realistic time will help you be successful. Is it different on different days? Be thoughtful and realistic about this. Are Wednesdays just insane? Give yourself permission from the get-go to skip Wednesdays. Do not give yourself permission to let other things get in the way on the regular. If your daily time momagement goal is working out and, realistically, three days is all you can do, then only schedule yourself for three days. Daily just means more than once a week in time momagement language, so take it with a grain of salt and do what works for you. The important thing is that you actually do it.

Step 3

Repeat. Now do the same thing for your weekly and annual goals.

For the annual goal, chances are it's something big like a job change or vacation. Put an end date on your calendar of when you want to accomplish this. If it's a vacation, block out the dates you want to go. If it's a job change, select a target date you want to be at your next company. Again, be realistic. Don't expect to have a new job in a month if you haven't even updated your resume or know the direction or industry you're leaning towards.

Did that feel easy? It should have. The harder part will actually be executing these tasks. The good news is, you're about 20 steps closer. You're well on your way to becoming a badass time momager. Give yourself a high five, or a clap because that's basically what a self-high is. Woohoo!

If you're not celebrating right now, it's because you might be having a hard time finding the time to schedule these things into your calendar. Did I hit the nail on the head? Are you looking at your schedule and making excuses for every single time slot you see? Or are you already talking yourself out of committing because you've failed before, know your daily life is a shit show that never goes as planned, or any other lame excuse why you won't even give yourself the pep talk to do this exercise?

I know that was a tad harsh, but let me ask you a few simple questions then.

If your kid was sick and had to go to the doctor, would you make time to take him?

If your husband's boss was coming over for dinner tomorrow night, would you make time to clean your house?

30

If your manager gave you an urgent project to work on due by Friday or the company would lose a lot of money, which would, in turn, affect your bonus, would you make time to complete it?

I think I've proven you wrong. Time is what you make of it. So, if those goals are really important to you, make the time on your calendar right now as your first step in doing them. Remember, you are worthy of it. If these goals aren't that important, choose ones that are and get to it.

Strategies to Execute

Ok, I was a little tough on you before, but now I want to share with you my soft side because:

A. I'm a Gemini.
and
B. I'm human.

First off, be prepared for hiccups, roadblocks, challenges, and real life shit that is going to get in your way. Even when I do this exercise with all good intentions and try to stick to the plan, life happens. My train gets delayed. My kid gets sick. My hubs has to work late. You know the deal.

I want you to remember this:

If you can't actually execute something on your calendar because of a major work crisis or a sick kid or anything else that life throws you, immediately reschedule it. Don't beat yourself up. Shit happens. Just reschedule it, preferably, within the next

24 hours. The calendar police are not going to come for you. Just remember, nothing changes if nothing changes. So, hold yourself accountable for still making it happen. You are in charge here, no matter what curve ball life throws at you.

Next, stop saying, "I don't have time" and replace it with "It's not a priority to me."

Seriously, just changing this simple saying impacted my life in a major way. I used to say, "I don't have time to work out." In reality, the truth was (and still is) most days, when I think of all the things I want to focus my energy on, going to a gym doesn't make the list. I know, and trust me, one day I hope this isn't the case for me personally, but for right now, it's my reality. When I started saying, "Working out isn't a priority to me," it made me feel less like a phony or like I was making excuses not to work out and more comfortable with the fact that I was making a conscious decision not to work out.

Honestly, it was really liberating! I'm still active and I still find ways to squeeze short stretches of exercises into my day, but taking a sweaty spin class or going on a five mile run like I used to do doesn't make the cut these days. And that's totally ok with me for now. If something is not a priority to you, then don't let it nag you and focus on something else. Recognizing this is a good first step. If something is a priority, you will realize it as soon as you start using the phrase "It's not a priority to me," instead of "I don't have time." Saying this will make you feel icky and not sit well. It will be your kick in the ass to ignite change in what you're doing and make it a priority. So, ask yourself, what's more of a priority? Sleeping that extra half hour or working out? Getting that promotion or spending time with your baby? You are the only one who *can* and *needs* to decide that here. I never said it was fair or easy, but you've got a certain amount of control over this, so decide and do it.

When it comes to the bigger ticket items, break it down, mama—and I don't mean on the dance floor, you don't want to pull a muscle! Break it down into small, actionable steps you can take and schedule immediately. Steps that are going to get you closer to that major accomplishment.

For example, if your annual time momagement goal is changing jobs, schedule 30 minutes on Tuesday to work on your resume, 10 minutes each day to add connections on your LinkedIn, 30 minutes a week to reach out to recruiters, and so on. This is going to make that big goal feel more attainable and give you the time to feel like you're getting closer with each step you take. The smaller you can break these steps down, the more likely it is you are going to actually complete them because they are going to feel way less intimidating.

Finally, especially if you're having a hard time scheduling overall, do the Three Day Test. For three days, write down how you spend every minute using my Three Day Test sheet in the back of this book. Where are the gaping holes? Where are you potentially wasting your time? Where could you be multitasking? I say multitasking lightly because not all tasks can be multitasked, but some most definitely can. Use those times to schedule your time momagement goals. You'll probably be pretty damn surprised by what you find. Trust me. If you're not having a hard time scheduling and are an over-achiever, do this exercise too. Maybe you'll find you have even more time than you think or maybe you'll notice where you want to make time for other things that are more important to you.

A Word on Multi-Tasking

Multitasking should not be something you're doing all day, every day. Multitasking can be helpful when momaging your time, but it isn't a necessity, and it shouldn't happen in all instances. When you're spending time doing a task that requires your full attention, you should *not* be multitasking. For example, when you're playing with your kid, you shouldn't also be answering e-mails or checking your social media. Chances are you're doing a pretty shitty job playing Legos if you're trying to respond to that email at the same time. Don't do a half-assed job at something important to you. Multitasking inevitably pulls some part of your brain away from both tasks you're trying to complete, so if either of those items are important enough to you, give your full attention to one before jumping to another, even if it's just for five or 10 minutes.

Multitasking is a reality for me, but I only do it in some cases, and I recommend you do the same. For example, a big time of my day that I multitask is my commute. I ride public transportation, so it's super easy for me to be able to multitask while I'm on the train. I do a lot of things during that time each day. Sometimes, it's cut and dry productive things I need to get done, like ordering necessities on Amazon or paying bills. Other times, it's doing something more for me, like listening to a podcast or audiobook. The thing I don't like to do during my commute time is to scroll my social media for 40 minutes and waste that time. Will I occasionally scroll? Absolutely. I'm normal. But it's done sparingly and intentionally, most times.

Another area I'll often multitask is while folding laundry or doing a mundane house task. I'll try and call a friend while doing these things, so it serves a dual purpose: cultivating a relationship with a friend and getting something tedious and necessary done, like cleaning up the kitchen. It's also making that shitty task feel less shitty because I'm not even thinking about it as I catch up with a friend on the latest happenings in her life.

When it comes to multitasking, choose wisely. Solo-task the mindful and multitask the mindless. If you reverse those, you'll start to feel like you're losing your mind because you'll be far from the Zen place of balance, achievement, and completion you're on a quest for. If you need your brain to feel complete, don't multitask and cheat.

Let's Recap

- Your time momagement goals are crucial in providing clarity in how you want to spend your time. Your list should be super clear and easy to measure.
- Choose a daily, weekly, and annual time momagement goal to start.
- Find the best calendar solution for you and schedule your goals into your life.
- If you're having a hard time doing so, take the Three Day Test in the back of this book. If you're not, take the Three Day Test anyway.
- Multitask the mindless. Solo-task the mindful. Tasks that don't require your full attention should be multitasked. Tasks that do require your full attention shouldn't.

Chapter 3

Make Time Your B

"Either you run the day or the day runs you."
-Jim Rohn

In this chapter you'll learn to:

- Identify who or what motivates you.
- Pinpoint who or what demotivates you.
- Take control of your time, even in situations you can't control.
- Find your communication style and learn about other types as well.

Ah, motivation. She's the best thing that can happen to you. She helps you do incredible things. So, in this chapter, you're going to get to know her, become her friend, invite her over, make her coffee, and let her stay awhile. She is the one who is going to help you through this. So, be very, *very* nice to her.

Everyone's motivation is different, just like everyone's BFF is different. What's yours? Is it a person? Your kids? Your spouse? Is it your college body? Your former abs? Or ass? My college body was not necessarily hotter by the way, but that's another story. Is it moving into a bigger house? Is it buying your first house? Whatever motivation looks like to you, get down with her and make her a big part of your life because *she* is going to be the one who helps you when shit gets real.

Are you a social butterfly? Basically, do you have a lot of BFFs or a lot of different motivators in this case? That's ok! Hell, that's even better. Your motivational tribe is going to keep you going, as long as you surround yourself with them as much as possible. They are your biggest fans, your cheerleading squad, that little angel on your shoulder telling you to do the right thing when you're faced with the sinful plague of doing something you *want* to do with your time versus wasting that time away.

Before you read any further, I want you to pause and think about who or what your motivators, or as I like to call them- your lovers, are right now. Make a list of them and keep it handy because you're going to be referencing these things or people often.

Your lovers are going to become part of your daily routine if they're not already. They're going to be your cheerleaders when you're still miles from the finish line. They're going to pick you up when you fall. They're going to bring you water when you're out of breath and wine when you're out of patience. And finally, they're going to give you a hug when you feel like giving up followed by a firm smack on the ass to tell you to get back up and do it again.

Here are my motivators, aka my lovers:

1. My kids
2. Motivational quotes or affirmations
3. Inspiring authors and entrepreneurs like Brené Brown and Marie Forleo
4. My life coach and other mentors I've had in the past
5. Positive feedback from followers or fans or friends
6. Financial success

A word about financial success, or my number six motivator above: financial success isn't really specific enough of a motivator for me, and it shouldn't be for you either. I know, in my mind, what financial success looks like: it's a double, stainless steel oven in a gorgeous kitchen, three to four vacations per year, working on my own terms and schedule, and yes, bringing in a certain dollar amount each year (that's for my eyes only-sorry). If this is a motivator for you too, then paint a clear picture of what that means to you. Is it a number in your bank account? A four-bedroom vacation home in Florida? A navy-blue E-class Mercedes with tan leather interior? Carrara marble tops in your kitchen? These are necessary to articulate in order to fully envision what financial success looks like in your life. Clarity, just like in your time momagement goals, is crucial to keep your financial success, or any other motivation, going. So, envision that beautiful car parked in your driveway with a big red bow on it and make *that* your visual.

It's not only important to know who or what your lovers are. You need to also keep them close to you, like your kids at the mall during the mad rush of the holiday season. Here are some things I like to do to keep my motivators with me as often as humanly possible:

1. Make my desktop background at work a really cute picture of my kids
2. Make my phone background something similar or an inspiring quote
3. Listen to audiobooks from my favorite authors on my commute
4. Follow things that lift me up and don't bring me down on social media
5. Read love mail from people I've inspired
6. Set financial goals and equate them to actual things to purchase (*i.e. When we hit this number in the bank, we'll renovate our kitchen or take that vacation to Hawaii.*)

Since we don't live in Disneyland and this is real freakin' life, there are often toxic beings or things that try to dull our motivational sparkle. These little suckers can be huge distractors and consequently, time sucks. I've heard some people call them "time-sucking vampires" because they literally suck the life out of you. I like to call them-you guessed it-haters.

Haters Gonna Hate

Just like knowing what/who your motivators are, it's important to know what/who your demotivators are, or as we'll keep referring to them in this book, your haters. If you're visualizing your high school nemesis who you haven't seen in 10 or even 20 years right now as your hater, let me take a moment to broaden this image for you. While Jenna Kauffman may be a total hater, she's likely not your only one, or even your most relevant one when it comes to time momagement. And by the way, Jenna Kauffman was *not* my high school nemesis. In fact, I don't even know who you are, fictional Jenna, so if you're reading this book, no hard feelings.

Here are your haters—the things or people that are currently and likely getting in the way of your motivation:

TV: I was recently at a birthday party chatting it up with a group of fellow moms. The conversation shifted toward TV shows: The Bachelor, The Bachelor in Paradise, Southern Charm, the list goes on. Now, I won't sit on my high, cableless horse here and shame anybody for watching TV. I also watch TV. I am human after all. And a very wise and successful C-level executive once told me, "The brain needs a break sometimes." Mindless TV definitely does that for me. It gives my brain a break. But I'd be lying if I didn't tell you watching TV is huge time waster, aka a hater. According to Wikipedia, the average American spends about four hours per day watching TV. Four hours! Now if you're feeling good after reading that statistic because you barely spend half that time watching TV daily, then good for you. But realistically, mama, that's still two hours of totally available time you could be spending doing something from your time momagement list.

Social-effing-media: Have you ever gone so far down the social media rabbit hole when you come up for air you can't even remember how you got down there to begin with? You know how this goes. You opened the app to literally check one thing, and 45 minutes later you're on your eighth-grade boyfriend's baby mama's page watching her gender reveal video from four years ago? I'm not proud of that moment. I let the social hater take over. The social hater knows you can't stop scrolling because as soon as you lose interest, she puts some magical ad or intriguing stranger in front of you so you can't take your eyes away—total hater.

Negative Nellies or Patties or Jessicas: These people will literally suck every ounce of happiness, enthusiasm, motivation, and confidence you have out of you. They will create, water and grow the plant of self-doubt in you and make you believe the new normal is their negative, drama-filled, soap opera life. Don't be fooled. They tend to crack jokes about their lack of motivation and achievements. They set the bar low and ridicule anyone who goes above it. Beware of these haters. They're wolves in sheeps' clothing, imitation Guccis, talk-behind-your-back-not-ever-really-happy-for-you-bitches.

Self-doubt: See above. Typically, Nelly, Patty or Jessica rubs off on you and causes a negative and doubtful you to grow deep inside. You begin questioning every single thing you were once excited about. You begin questioning everything in general. Do you even like the color pink? Hell yes, you like pink. Pink is your fucking color. Only a hater would hate pink.

Excuses: I'm too busy. I feel guilty. I'm exhausted all the time. I need a friend to do that with. Blah blah blah blah blah. There will always be an excuse, just like there will always be a hater. Tell that bitch to shut it and then get back to business. You ain't got no time or space for the excuse hater in your world.

Girlfriend, let me tell you something you've probably heard before, especially if you're a fan of 90s rap like me: *haters gonna hate*. Don't let haters kick motivation out of your space. They are going to try and bring you downtown, Julie Brown. Misery loves company, so make sure you don't get sucked into this negativity. Remember, it's better to be alone and happy than hangin' with a group of haters. And really, are you ever alone if you have your BFF motivation with you? I don't think so.

I hate to keep up the hater talk, but I've got to share this one last thing with you because *the more you know* (hums commercial melody and envisions shooting star before reading on). A while back I saw this quote, and it really resonated with me. I used to feel super self-conscious about my million and one ideas and often wouldn't share them because I was worried about what the haters would think. Then I read this:

"Have you ever met a hater doing better than you?

Me neither."

I thought about it, of course, because you know me and my analytical brain. I'm not sure if truer words have ever been spoken. By the way, whoever did speak this truth bomb, I owe you a lot. Haters don't want you to do better because it only further highlights what losers they are. A hater holds you down. A lover lifts you up. A hater is jealous. A lover is genuinely happy for you. A hater complains. A lover preaches. When I thought about my haters, this quote instantly resonated. Not one hater person, hater feeling, or hater thing was any better than me. They were far worse. I like to think of myself as someone who doesn't think she's better than anyone else, except my haters. I'm better than that, if not for the sheer reason that I don't bring other people down. When I figured out this life lesson, it was as though the lightbulb of good lighting went on, posted me into a beautiful, confident Instagram filtered photo and I haven't looked back since. I hope you'll feel the same once you start realizing how insignificant and so-not-at-your-level your haters are, mama.

Now that you've got motivation on speed dial and your haters in check, you're going to start working your time. You're going to start showing her who's in charge, making her your B, telling her like it is...and like it ain't. So, get ready mom boss, because you're about to get real bossy.

Organization Is Key

You've heard this before, and you're going to hear it again from me: being organized is key. Planning is not only essential, but it's also crucial if you want to see any of those items on your list *actually happen*. And yes, I'm talking anything from planning a vacation to planning to get eight hours of sleep that night. The thing is, and I can say this because I tend to think of myself as a Ph.D. Planner (yeah, that's a thing), you also need to know when to be a little laid back about all these plans, with your mind on your time and your time on your mind, of course. I told you I like 90s rap.

Even if you don't think you're super organized, chances are you're rocking some level of organization, or you wouldn't be

44

able to leave your house daily. Getting to work on time, having a successful trip to the park with your littles, or even cooking dinner for your crew requires some type of organization. I'm sure people have said to you before, "I don't know how you do it." You should consider this a total compliment to your organized self, even if it comes from your lazy, single, can't-get-her-shit-together cousin. Don't ever doubt that you aren't kicking ass every single day. You absolutely are.

What you're probably also feeling, though, is a sense of inadequacy, a feeling like you're not getting the things done that you wish you had the time for. The harsh truth is that on most days, something's going to give. Something won't fit in. Something won't go as planned. That something doesn't always need to be you. And that something sometimes *can* make the time cut, along with everything else. Those days are called winning, but you can't expect to be winning every day. As I said, we don't live in Disneyland.

Perfectionism

It's really hard when you're a Type-A planner to accept when things, well, don't go as planned. You can feel deflated or like you're not nailing this thing called life unless you've checked everything off your list that day. But the harsh reality of life is that many times, things *don't* go as planned. You know who taught me that? Kids. And I'll add another layer: boy kids. My mom literally laughed out loud when she heard I was having twin boys, which I actually think is kind of mean, but that's for my therapist, not you. I say this with all the love in the world I have for my children. Kids throw you off track, a lot. And boys, well, they turn into men. And we all know most times us ladies

45

are the more organized ones in the house (at least that's the case for my house and 99% of all my girlfriends too).

When my twins were born, I had planned their birthday (aka I had scheduled a C-section). I told you I was a planner. Yet, this was also the safer option with my high-risk pregnancy since delivering past that date could have resulted in serious complications. Let's get back to the story, though. Two and half weeks earlier than their scheduled birthday, those boys decided they didn't like that plan and showed up to the party early. We were in the middle of renovating our newly purchased house and hadn't even moved in. We were living in my old bedroom at my dad's house, literally out of suitcases. I knew my twins would be spending some time in the NICU, so in the course of a week, we moved ourselves into our home, quarantining ourselves to our kitchen, dining room, and living room (yes, we all slept in the dining room for the first month). It was not ideal, especially when people wanted to visit. It also wasn't how I had planned it. But, we had two healthy kids, our first adult home, and we were incredibly close to the kitchen for all those nighttime feedings. Silver lining.

So, what did I learn and have to become more comfortable with? What did two tiny humans teach me from the day they prematurely arrived into this world? What life lesson did my post-partum days of healing and strength and acceptance throw at me? At the end of the day, it's *not* all going to be perfect, or essentially, go as planned. And, here's the most important part. And, that's ok. It was ok. It was more than ok because it taught me another life lesson, as all these non-planned moments do. It taught me to be more flexible, more tolerant, more patient, more focused on the bigger picture, more capable of displaying a mature, resilient, and incredibly strong example for the VIPs I had just welcomed to my life.

It Won't Always Be Perfection, and That's Okay

By all means, this wasn't an easy concept for me to grasp. I'm a fixer, a doer, a productivity perfectionist. I'm sure you've been there. You finally get your newborn babies fed, changed, buckled into their car seats and then one throws up and the other has a diaper blowout, making you 20 minutes late for their well visit at the pediatrician, while you're also wearing a shirt that has more bodily fluid on it than Monica Lewinsky's famous blue dress. Also, your shoes don't match, and you haven't washed your hair in like a week. Even if all you wanted to do that day was shower and get to this doctor's appointment on time and you did neither, remember: it's not all going to go as planned, *and that's ok.*

So, here's what you need to do now that have you this golden nugget of knowledge. Decide what *is* attainable and what will still make you feel good. For example, if one of your time momagement goals is to workout daily, but realistically you can't do a daily workout, how about working out three times a week? Or taking a 20-minute power walk during your lunch break? Or, shit, what about taking the stairs instead of the escalator or elevator? These should all make you feel like you're making progress, even if it's not perfection. These are steps in the right direction and, most importantly, these are enough, mama.

Ever hear that expression, "Practice makes perfect"? I know I heard it ad nauseam growing up. I even find myself saying it to my kids as they learn to write their letters. It's almost annoying, yet undeniably true. It's like a rite of passage. Everyone says it, and everyone believes it. But, as a recovering perfectionist, why would I want to be perfect? Why would I want to go back to that deep, dark place?

Hold up, don't think I'm basically backtracking on everything I just said to you about not trying to be perfect. What I mean here is the more you do something, the more habitual and easy and normal it's going to feel. For example, we all know crash dieting works only for the short-term. Yeah, I can lose those five pounds to fit into that dress I want to wear to my cousin's wedding in two weeks. But realistically, I'm probably going to eat and drink enough that same weekend to have gained those five pounds right back. The only *real* way to lose weight and keep it off is changing habits! We have to change the type of food we are eating or the amount of food we are eating. We have to start working out or add to our current work-out routine. It's a lot of practice to reach that "perfect" or in this case, that target weight and, most importantly, keeping it there.

Here's an even more compelling statistic for you. It takes a solid 21 days to form a new habit. You need to do something over and over and over again (plus another 18 more times) to make that an official part of your routine. So, keep up the practice. It will pay off, I promise.

When I talk about that 'perfect' that comes from plenty and plenty of practice, what I really mean is, have you put *everything* into making this change, fitting this goal into your life, and prioritizing it to feel like you are making progress? If the answer is yes, you've done your job. You can trust that with continued effort, you are not only going to get to the mecca of where you want to be, you may already be there. You're on the right path, the correct exit, the fortuitous journey you're meant to be on. Consequently, you should feel all the feels, mama.

Putting everything, however, into making that time momagement goal happen doesn't mean you should hit the ground running with anything and everything you can possibly do all at once. This causes burnout and, most times, leads to quitting. Start small, change one thing at a time. If it is losing those pounds, begin with adding 15 minutes of walking to your day. You can fit 15 minutes in, no matter how little 'free time' you have. Park further away. Take your dog for a walk. Ask your colleague if you can have a walking meeting. Walk while you're doing something else, like making a phone call. If you're an over-achiever, you may even do 20 minutes some days and feel even better. Do it for 21 days. Then add something else to your weight loss plan. Is this a slower way to get there? Yes. Is it similarly a more sustainable long-term solution? Also, yes. Moral of the story: slow and steady wins the race. Fast and furious crashes and burns. You can keep your momentum without going from 0 to 100.

A Word about Control

As moms, we have control over a lot of things. Many of us are the managers at home and often at work too. We're in charge of a lot of details, from what everyone in the house eats to what type of toothpaste they brush their teeth with. It's exhausting, yet also feels so familiar, normal, and downright comfortable to have all that control. It causes us to be somewhat 'control freaks.' But, it's not our fault!

I hate the word control freak. It makes me feel like a, well, freak. According to Google, a freak is defined as "a very unusual and unexpected event or situation or a person, animal, or plant with an unusual physical abnormality." I am neither of these nor do I think the term is very nice, quite frankly. So many of us moms fit this category though, and not just because of our personalities, but because by default we *need* to take control.

The important, and often hard, pill to swallow when it comes to control is this: no matter how much you want to control it, all of it, you likely can't. Ahh! So, then the million-dollar question becomes this. What do you do in situations when you really don't have control of your time? How can you make time your B, when sometimes she's out of your control? Don't fret, mama. Just like those bigger goals, there are smaller scale parts that you *can* control. Phew! I can hear you breathing a sigh of relief through these pages. Having some level of control is going to make you feel *that much better* because control is something we as moms pretty much *need to have* to survive in the mom jungle of life.

There are lots of things I can think of when it comes to a lack of control on the time front.

Here are the top three that stand out.

1. Work
2. Traffic/Commute
3. Hubs' schedule

What about you? Does this list resonate? Could you add to it? Write that shit down. All of it. Because we're about to go deep on how we can tame those uncontrollable time beasts.

Remember, in this chapter we're making time our B. There are going to be times when you're going to have to domesticate the time animal because she's out of control. She's sabotaging your hard work and efforts. She's shitting all over your perfectly planned schedule. She's not letting *you* be in control of your time.

Start with getting to a better headspace. This is so damn important, as it will lead the way for the rest of your actions to follow. If you're in a funk about the areas of your life mentioned above that are constantly messing up your time game, get pumped because you're about to walk all over it, in a very catwalk, New York fashion week, confident runway model sort of way.

Have you ever tried to plan for every possible issue that could come up to get somewhere on time with your toddler only to find that he throws a tantrum and makes his 30-pound-self feel like 200 as you try to peel him up off the floor, while wrestling to put his shoes on, and having your hair (which you spent 20 minutes actually doing that morning) look like you either just went through a hurricane, had crazy sex, or haven't brushed it in two years? I have. Taming the time beast (or toddler beast) ain't easy. But you can do it.

From a time perspective, here's a good example. When it comes to work, I can't just decide I don't want to work nine hours a day. It's my job. It's the expectation. And we need two salaries in my house, so this isn't a viable option. The key here is to ask yourself, "What do I have control over to make time?"

Can I ask for an earlier or later schedule, so I can spend more time with my kids when they're awake?

Can I work from home one or more days a week to avoid commute times?

Can I ask for a 10/40 or a 9/80 schedule?

Can I become a freelancer and make my own hours?

No idea is too far-fetched. Thinking outside the box when you're trying to tame the time beast is the best way to get to the right end result. Don't be afraid to get super creative here. Write down anything and everything that comes to mind, even if it seems unattainable right then and there. Almost every time I came up with a crazy idea, it ended up morphing into something executable, even in situations where I didn't have control of my time.

Here's the most important ingredient you need to add to your time control casserole. You need to be strategic. You need to plan. You need to be organized. Remember that important mantra I preach about?

Let's talk planning on some of these examples I just threw out there with regards to work. If you're asking for more flexibility at work, you absolutely need to be strategic about this. Don't let your emotions get the best of you. Don't make this about you, even though it is. You can't walk into your boss' office (no matter how great a relationship you think you have) with welled up, tearful eyes and say, "This is too hard, and I need things to change around here because I'm falling apart." Don't. Do. It.

I don't know about you, but my boss wouldn't give my request more than three seconds of thought before saying a pretty firm N-O if I presented it like that. And by the way, I actually really like my boss. She's a mom and she's fairly understanding. I'd say, 80% of the time we see eye to eye. But I'm not an idiot either. I also know my boss' job is to think about the bigger picture for the company. Her job is *not* to care about my feelings or lack of time. Harsh, I know, but also true.

So, you need to "sell' your request to her in hopes that she'll "buy" it. You need to ask yourself, "What's in it for her? For the company? What is going to make her review this request and see the value, the benefit, the no brainer reason why she should approve it?"

Be strategic. Think about what's valuable to your boss. Think about what she cares about. Think about things that make life easier for her, that make her look good to her boss, and that would give her what she needs, not what you need (even though yes, this is ultimately about you).

Here's how you might present this request:

Step 1

Make a list of all the pros—why this idea makes sense for the company *and* for your boss. Take yourself out of your head for a minute and put yourself in your boss' stilettos. WIIFH-what's in it for her? Ask yourself, "What reasons can I give her that she can't possibly turn down making this happen for me because they are *that good?*"

For example:

Does it help with call volume or customer support in a different time zone?

Does it offer more support to colleagues in the office or remotely?

Does your role require more strategic thought and planning or creative tasks that are better done at home with fewer distractions?

Are you more productive during those earlier or later hours and your output will be better?

Can you manage something more easily from home that she would love to delegate?

And finally, does it mean better work/life balance for you as a valuable employee?

Make your last line item something that says this will help you too. You don't want your request to appear unauthentic. So, if it does mean having a better work/life balance, say it. Just don't make it the most important priority for making the request.

Step 2

Don't forget the cons. It is *crucial* to show you have thought about this from all ends, not only the positive ones. So, add a list of cons. Again, be strategic about this. You need to list more pros than cons (obviously). You should also add a note of how you can fix the problem before it potentially even surfaces—or at least verbally present this part when you review with your boss.

For example:

Potential con #1: letting you work remotely more often might mean other people will request this as well and form a remote epidemic in your office.

Followed by your proposed fix:

"I've been with the company xx years and with tenure and seniority, maybe this is something that could be offered only to me for those reasons?"

OR

"I totally get how that could impact other people; that's fair. I'd be happy to come up with a remote working document that outlines the company's expectations on this policy if this is something that will be offered across the board."

Potential con #2: lack of support in the office if you're working odd hours or from home.

Followed by your proposed fix:

"I know this is a big change and can understand not having my role physically here every day or during traditional hours will be different. So many companies are moving toward remote employees, so they have a wider range of talent that isn't necessarily local to tap into. I did some research on these

Marisa Volpe Lonic

products that would be great ways to maintain communication with my team throughout the work day so they still know I'm present and available for support (give examples of Skype, Slack, Zoom, etc.). I also recently read an article about how working at times when you have optimal brain power (not necessarily nine to five) makes you xx% more efficient and productive at work and wanted to share it with you."

Step 3

Sell it. I'm going to tell you the most important thing I've learned when it comes to sales, and really, when it comes to life in general if you want anyone to listen to you. You need to communicate your message in the right way, and the right way isn't always the same for every situation or every person. In fact, it can be very, very different.

There are four main types of communication styles, and we all have one category that we fit into best. This is the one that feels most comfortable, comes most naturally, and is most often the way we tend to communicate. It's like our comfort zone, our security blanket. It's my Long Island accent that comes out after a few drinks. It's the way you tend to communicate when you're not putting forth much effort or energy toward your audience because you're just being you and keeping it real. Fist pump.

I've studied these styles a lot and have come up with my own interpretations of what they mean for us mamas. Before I tell you more about what these styles are though, I want you to take a few minutes and take this short quiz. I know, it sort of feels like you're 17 again and reading Cosmopolitan, but who didn't love taking those quizzes back in the day? So, go ahead and

56

warp yourself back to Y2K for a minute and take the short quiz on the next page. You'll be happy you did.

Find Your Communication Style

1. Your kid's teacher requests a parent-teacher conference regarding your son's behavior. What's your first reaction?
   A. You e-mail her back and schedule it immediately for that afternoon, talk with your kid about it, and create a positive discipline chart at home.
   B. You e-mail her back and schedule for later in the week, ask some questions in your message, and buy a book on positive discipline to learn more about the concept.
   C. You call her and schedule the meeting—you want to connect and hear her voice. Then you ask your mom friends more about positive discipline.
   D. You e-mail her back to schedule for later in the week and start thinking of ways you can improve the issue. Maybe an incentive chart or maybe more one on one time or maybe a family vacation?

2. Your husband tells you his company was acquired, and he consequently got laid off. What's your first reaction?
   A. "Let me jazz up your LinkedIn profile for you. You'll be interviewing by Friday."
   B. "What happened? What's the severance package? Can you apply to another role within the company? I'm going to Google the acquisition, hang on."
   C. "Oh no, babe. I am so sorry. Are you ok? What can I do to help? Do you want a beer? Or a back rub? I'll contact my friend who's a recruiter to help you out."
   D. "Let's talk about it. How about a career change? You always said you wanted to go into sales…"

3. You just found what you thought was *the* best deal on a pair of shoes at Nordstrom. You get to check-out and, the salesperson says they were mismarked. What do you do?
   A. Make a quick decision, and that decision is YES. Pull out your credit card and don't look back.
   B. Step offline, take out your phone and do a search online to see if you can find the shoes cheaper elsewhere, contemplate for a bit while you look at other shoes, then decide to buy them. It makes sense.
   C. Call your bestie, describe the shoes heel to toe, tell her how amazing they make you feel, then buy them because she convinces you that you deserve them.
   D. Imagine yourself wearing the shoes on vacation, with your husband in Paris, or even on date night this Friday in the city. I mean, you could even wear these babies to preschool pickup, and it would change your day. Sold.

4. The pediatrician tells you that your kid isn't hitting all the milestones at 18-months-old. Which best sounds like you?
   A. You Google the milestones, schedule a meeting with your nanny and come up with an action plan on practicing them daily—all before leaving the parking lot.
   B. You research milestones on various websites that evening, sleep on it, talk with your husband and ultimately conclude that you think your kid is fine, but if things don't change in two months, you'll revisit the issue.

C. You hug your baby, call your mom, and cry a little. Then you contact a developmental expert to come over and evaluate.

D. You make a list of questions for Google and find some new parenting concepts and theories. After reading up on this, you realize that milestone measurement is different everywhere and you're going to start parenting in a more Swedish fashion.

5. It's Moms' Night Out and your turn to plan. What do you do?

A. Make a reservation immediately at the hot spot that you've been dying to get into since it opened. Then you send everyone an Evite with the details.

B. Do a YELP search and compare three places' star ratings before deciding. Choose the one that has the highest ratings, is in a convenient location, and serves the best margaritas.

C. Ask everyone what they're in the mood for via group text. Once you have a consensus on Mexican food, get a recommendation from your colleague and make a reservation. It also helps that your colleague's brother is the manager. Possible free dessert?

D. Brainstorm something unique and different, change your mind, then choose a restaurant you've always wanted to try, even though it may be a little outside the box, but everyone should still like.

6. Your best friend tells you she's getting a divorce. What's your first reaction?

A. "I'm so sorry. What do you need? An attorney? A girls' getaway? A dating profile on E-Harmony? I'll make it happen for you."

B. "I'm so sorry. Tell me everything. Did he cheat? Is there proof? My colleague just got a divorce, and these are steps she followed to ensure she ended up financially ok."
C. "I'm so sorry, honey. I can't even imagine what you must be feeling. It's ok to just cry. I'm here for you."
D. "I'm so sorry. That's so shocking. I always thought you and John were so happy. I mean you guys were always smiling in your pics on Instagram. I've heard of these new divorce mediators who are great for amicable divorces. You should find one!"

7. You find out that there's a promotion opening up at work and it's an area of the business you are really interested in. What does your strategy look like?
A. Work on a proposal pitch for your boss and schedule a time to chat asap. You don't want them to start of thinking of anyone but you for that role.
B. Research the salary, expectations, and schedule. Plan out if it makes sense for you from all areas of life to opt-in for this role. Then put together a fact-based proposal of why you're right for the job.
C. Talk to your husband, your mom, and your best friend about it. Your people always give you good advice and will help you decide if you should go for it.
D. Look at your astrology notes and see if a job change was in the stars for you this year.

The Results

If you answered mostly A's…
You're a "Make it Happen" communicator. You do just that. You want action. You like to keep conversation short, direct, and want a result asap.

If you answered mostly B's…
You're a "How's That Work" communicator. You like facts, information, and understanding it all. You're pretty analytical and need all the details to move forward. Slow and steady wins the race for you.

If you answered mostly C's…
You're a "Love My Peeps" communicator. You like people, and you like to talk. You tap into your network on the regular for advice, experience, and support. Hearing a story about how that issue worked for your friend goes a long way with you.

If you answered mostly D's…
You're a "Think Outside the Box" communicator. You're full of ideas and like to explore creative and sometimes farfetched solutions. You like to look at the bigger picture, not only the issue at hand. Sometimes you take the long road, but it gets you there nonetheless.

Most times, the person we're talking to doesn't fall into the same category as us.

So, maybe you're a *How's That Work* communicator, and your boss is a *Make It Happen* communicator. You're usually talking to your boss in your comfy *How's That Work* style, but with her primary *Make It Happen* zone, she's not interpreting the message exactly the way you want her to. Why? Because she's got a different communication style. She's likely growing impatient with your wordiness and has tuned you out by the 60-second mark. Ugh! That's so not the result you were hoping for, and definitely not worth all the time and effort you put into prepping this request. What an epic fail!

So, what do you need to do to be a good communicator and get the result you were hoping for? It's really easy. You need to adjust your style to fit the person you're talking to. Cue the gospel music: Hallelujah! In this case, get to the point a hell of a lot faster, stress the end results, use dates and actionable, tangible items. This is the kind of stuff that is going to make a *Make It Happen* boss swoon and hopefully take you up on your offer.

I bet you're probably already doing this to a certain degree in a lot of situations. Think about it. Do you talk to your husband the same way you talk to your son's preschool teacher? Or your best friend the same way you talk to the cashier at Costco? You're already used to altering the way you talk and words you use in your day-to-day life. Now, you just have the added knowledge and understanding of how to adjust your communication style on top of it.

Think about the important peeps you talk to on the daily. Think about what would happen if you made a slight change in how you spoke to them. Would your message be better received? Think about what type of communication language they speak, and then speak their language. That's it.

Let's Recap

- Know your motivators, or lovers, and keep them close.
- Identify your demotivators, or haters, and distance yourself.
- Practice makes perfect, and by perfect, I mean progress. Don't let perfectionism debilitate you.
- Figure out your communication style and adjust it to the person or situation you're talking to. Your conversation will be more likely to go in the direction you hoped it would.

Chapter 4

Form a Tribe

"Be strong enough to stand alone, smart enough to know when you need help, and brave enough to ask for it."
-Mark Amend

In this chapter, you'll learn:

- The best places or people to include in your tribe.
- Reasons why moms don't ask for help and how to feel less guilty about doing so.
- Tips and tricks on how to gain more support.

This chapter is all about getting more help. And before you say it out loud, in your head, sideways, frontways, in between ways, I want you to know that I know. I know what you're thinking. Asking for help, especially as a mom, can be *really hard*. Our internal mom self puts her hand out, like "Whoa, girl. Stop right there. You are supposed to be doing this all alone *and* making it look easy." Well, I'm here to tell you, "It just ain't true." You're welcome.

Asking for help can feel like a luxury, especially if it costs you money. This was a hard pill for me to swallow. Growing up, my parents were very frugal and hardly ever paid for a service they could do themselves. I'm not trying to go all 'my poor childhood' on you. I appreciate the hard work and the core values I grew up with. It shaped me. It was, however, also an internal battle I had to fight when I grew up. I had a hard time justifying certain expenses, like a cleaning service for example. I learned the semi-hard way, but I'm now proud to say I pay a fantastic woman, who is amazing at cleaning, every two weeks to clean my house. And I am guilt-free! I have not once thought about going back to doing this task myself.

You need to remember this. Your time is not a luxury; it's a necessity. I'm going to repeat that because it is *so damn important*. Your time is *not* a *luxury*. It is a *necessity*. Your time is your sanity. Your time is your devotion to parenting, to wifing. Your time is your sense of accomplishment. Your time is you living your best life as your best self.

In 2009, I got married and honeymooned in Thailand. It was an incredible place to visit and an amazing cultural experience, especially being young, in love, and with the person I would be spending the rest of my life with. If you've never been to Thailand, you should add it to your bucket list, or maybe your time momagement goal list. A big part of Thai culture is Thai massage. I love massage, so I pampered myself with one daily on my trip. I mean, why wouldn't I? They were super inexpensive and could be found basically anywhere we went: on the beach, at the mall, in the hotel, at the Buddhist temples—literally everywhere. I learned that in the Thai culture massage is viewed as a medicinal and healing necessity practiced regularly, not a luxurious indulgence. Massage wasn't reserved for the wealthy and was affordable for almost anyone. It was looked at as something *all* people did, and regularly did, to stay healthy. What a thought! I still wonder why the U.S. hasn't adopted this viewpoint on massage. The Thai massage in this story can be swapped for time in our mom world. As moms, we view "me-time" as this precious, luxurious, sporadic thing that for about 15 years while we're raising young kids, we just 'do without.' This is not sustainable nor is it healthy.

You know what is healthy? Having a support system in place so you don't have to do it all, lose your shit, have a mental breakdown, and then blame everyone else for it.

Yes, asking for help can sometimes be hard. It's the mom equivalent of a man asking for directions. Does that even happen anymore with GPS? Probably not. I digress. Asking for help makes us feel like we can't handle our lives. I mean seriously, shouldn't every woman out there be able to manage a kid (or a few of them), a career, a marriage, a household, and some friendships, all while looking good, eating organic, and rockin' some not-so-Mom jeans? NO! No, no, no, no, no. Not without some help along the way.

Some people take asking for help as a sign of weakness, but studies actually show it's the biggest sign of trust. For example, if I ask my manager for help with something, I convince myself she's probably thinking "she isn't competent" or "she can't do the job," when in reality what she's thinking is "she trusts me enough to ask for help." Interesting concept, right? The people you ask for help aren't going to look at you as being less of a mom, less of a wife, less of a friend, less of an employee, etc. In fact, they're likely going to feel important because you trust them enough to share this level of vulnerability with them. And they're likely going to feel closer to you as an individual because your perceived perfect self is more approachable, more relatable, and *more real*. Asking for help is a way for you to:

Get help and free up some of that precious, precious time

and

Strengthen a relationship or six (depending how much help you ask for, mama)

Dual purpose baby, and I know you're a multi-tasker!

Your Tribe: Who's Invited?

Did you ever hear the expression, it takes a village? Of course you have, and I hope you know how true this is. The thing is, your village should consist of people who help you feel more relaxed, at peace, and supported. Your village is yours. It can consist of whoever you want it to. If your village is stressing you out, move.

I'm going to discuss some village members below. Some are common, and some are not so common. Take what works for you. Leave what doesn't. I'm not offended. I won't ever know what you took and what you left. I'm basically just telling you what has worked for me in hopes it may also work for you.

The Husband or Partner

I don't know about you, but there's this unspoken stage of marriage or relationships that occurs about a week after you've brought your newborn home from the hospital where you kind of hate your husband or partner. It lasts anywhere from one month to when you are sleeping through the night again. Have you experienced that? No? Me neither. Ok, I'm lying. I absolutely did. If you say you didn't, well, I think you might be lying to yourself, or you may have just suppressed that memory because I bet it likely happened to you too. Blame it on the hormones, or the sleep deprivation, or even partially on a person who just doesn't understand the necessity of being ultra-proactive and helpful during the neediest time in your life as a mom.

With my second pregnancy, I got some help before this marriage attack bomb hit our household. If I didn't, I am not sure I'd still be married today. Ok, that's an exaggeration. But, for real, that newborn stage is a hard time to be happily married. I was going to a "Moms of Newborns" type group and heard about *The Five Love Languages*, a book by Gary Chapman that helps couples communicate better. A mom in our group who had just had her second baby basically preached about what many of us were experiencing, or had previously experienced—the *'hate your hubs'* newborn stage. Then, she told all of us to take the *Love Language* quiz, and I'm pretty sure every single woman in that room did that night. I know I did.

Even if you're not in this rocky stage in your relationship, this is still a good tool to check out. There's an online assessment that both you and your partner can take. By the way, my hubs was so not into this. I imagine many other guys might have the same reaction. I had to read the questions out loud to him and make it beyond easy for him to complete. So, don't get discouraged if your spouse or partner tells you this is stupid, a waste of his time, and that you shouldn't bother him while he's watching football.

When you take this quiz be prepared for someone to pull back the secret curtain of what your preferred love language is. Discovering this gem of information, how he needs to be communicated with and how you need to be communicated with, was like discovering a whole new world. The results were eye-opening. I was doing it all wrong, and so was he. This is similar to adjusting your communication style as we talked about earlier, remember? The awareness alone can be a total game changer in how you and your partner get along.

Most people tend to communicate in their own love language because that's what comes most naturally to them. I don't know about you, but my hubs and I are pretty different people personality wise. I'm way more assertive, outgoing, and strict. He's laid-back, introverted, and easy-going. We're pretty much communication opposites. But hey, Paula Abdul knew what she was talking about when she created the 80s hit song *Opposites Attract*. Side note-when I was four I told my mom I wanted to be the next Paula Abdul when she retired, and I grew up. Anyway, talking to my hubs in my own love language was getting me a whole lot of nothing, and it was the same for him. Resentment built, frustration followed, and the marriage valleys grew deeper during the rough patches of newborn nor'easters and toddler tornadoes.

So, what does all of this mean and why is this starting to feel like marriage therapy? Here's my point in all this (I have one, I promise). If you want help from your husband or partner, you need to talk to him in a way that shows you appreciate him and you love him. And here's the most important part, he needs to understand it as well. If you speak in your love language, you're going to get nowhere. If you speak in his, you're going to be amazed at how much smoother things go.

Ever hear the expression, "It's not what you say, it's how you say it?" This is living proof of that concept and *so damn important*. Change the way you are both communicating with each other. I guarantee you will see a change in your hubs' efforts in helping you out and understanding your needs.

The Kids

Kids as young as two years old thrive on feeling like they're helpful beings and contributing to the family. I also like to think giving responsibilities to kids helps shape them into contributing members of society, not to mention good partners, parents, employees, and overall good people.

When my third baby was born, I noticed the inevitable. My three-year-olds started acting out. My sleep deprived self was snapping left and right. This was always followed by guilt-ridden moments of self-reflection and internal promises to do better tomorrow. I was overwhelmed, exhausted, and feeling like somewhat of a mom-failure.

So, what did I do? You guessed it. I *Pinterested* the shit out of incentive charts and made some extremely creative DIY versions of my own. And then, three weeks later, when the novelty of that wore off, I called a parenting expert and discovered I had it all wrong.

Well, kind of.

I learned that extrinsic incentives are good for temporary relief or introduction to new behaviors. Remember the 21-day thing? But, intrinsic incentives are gold and are what you really need to make this concept stick. For example, instead of earning a treat or movie for ten stickers, maybe each sticker earns recognition or positive reinforcement and ten stickers get you growth and closer to being a 'big kid.'

Another good parenting tip I got from this expert: responsibility popsicle sticks. Are you scratching your head right now asking yourself, "What the hell are responsibility popsicle sticks?" Allow me to explain, mama. You write an age-appropriate responsibility on a popsicle stick. Ideally, you make a bunch of these, one stick for each responsibility. For my four-year-olds at the time, these included: making their bed, setting the table for dinner, clearing the table after dinner, helping prepare dinner, filling water glasses for everyone, etc. Each day, they chose a stick (or more), and those were their jobs that day. All members of the family had jobs they were responsible for. Of course, moms typically have the most jobs. The point is, feeling like an important and contributing family member is good for kids too, even little ones. Responsibilities shouldn't be solely reserved for adults.

Keep in mind, the first—oh probably ten times—you do this, it's going to be tough. Well actually, the first couple of times may be exciting, but then the novelty wears off, and your kids are basically not into it anymore. Stick with it (pun intended). Just like you need 21 days to form a habit, so do they. Keep it up!

Family and Friends

It's a given that if you live near grandparents, you have an easy button for someone to call when you need help—especially free help. Most grandparents are happy to help when it comes to childcare, and hopefully, you feel a familial sense of trust and non-guilt tapping into this freebie resource.

Grandparents, though, are not always accessible, able or the right people to care for your kids. They may not be local. They may not be well. Or they may not be awesome people like you and me. Those are the facts of life, aren't they?

Let's get creative with who and how you can tap into other resources if your easy button ain't working.

Years ago, I started a babysitting co-op in the local moms' group I was in. Remember, I moved to a new city when my twins were two years old, without the grandparents. I was fortunate enough to have an au pair who moved with us, but if you know anything about the au pair program, you know that for working parents your hours are usually tapped by Friday, so date nights may still be non-existent unless you have another source.

A babysitting co-op is exactly what it sounds like: a group of families takes turns hosting each other's children at their home so that the other parents can enjoy a few kid-free hours. It's best for these groups to remain on the smaller side because, in all honesty, who can handle that many kids with only a couple of adults? You rotate hosting on a schedule that works best for you: weekly, monthly, or even quarterly. Each set of parents gets one or more date nights in exchange for hosting a kid party at their house so others can enjoy some time with their partners. This can also work for you-time during the day if a date night is not what you need to do with this time—running errands solo? Getting a mani-pedi? Fill in the time with whatever makes sense to you, and then repay the favor to your mama friend.

The thing about a babysitting co-op is this: just because someone else has kids, maybe even kids the same age as you, doesn't mean you should automatically be friends with them and/or instantly trust them with your kids. I know I feel this way. Motherhood is definitely an unspoken bond, but it doesn't automatically make us besties.

When I started the co-op, I kept this front and center. I added a short survey each mom had to fill out before I paired her up with another mom or two. Some of the questions on that survey gathered the following info:

- *Are your kids about the same age? Will there be age appropriate toys at their home(s)? Will the kids want to play together?*

76

- *Are the parents people you trust and gel with? Do they have similar parenting philosophies when it comes to screen time, food choices, helicoptering vs. not? I have plenty of friends who I love and adore, but I probably wouldn't leave my kids at their house without me there. Just saying.*
- *Are these people that want and need the same thing you do? If your friend lives next door to her mother-in-law and never needs a sitter, then this is not a good option for you. This other mama's gotta want this as bad as you do, or you're going to feel like you're 'bothering' her when you ask for a swap, and you don't need any more guilt. You've got enough of that, girlfriend.*

Not sure where to start to tap into some of these resources you probably already have? Here are some steps you can take *right now*:

1. Research a local mom group. Go on Facebook, Nextdoor, Google, whatever, and find one. They're everywhere. Some are even niche markets exclusively for moms of multiples or moms with special needs kids. Just find one and join.

2. If that group doesn't have a babysitting co-op, start one. I did. I guarantee your new mom friends will appreciate it.

3. Think about your current friends. Who pops into your head when you ask yourself the questions listed above about being a good fit to do this swap with? Then write her, or them, this email:

Hey mama,

How's it going? I was thinking of a way to have more date nights, and I thought of you since I know this is something you'd appreciate as well!

Would you be open to doing a babysitting swap once a month with me (and friend if applicable)? It would be a <u>Saturday night pizza and a movie</u> (or insert what makes sense here) at your house or mine for our kids so we could have a date night with our hubs when it's not our turn to host.

Let me know...I think this makes a lot of sense for both of us!

XO-Me

Doesn't get any easier than that. A quick copy/paste and a few edits and you've got yourself some kid-free time for a date night or time to do something for yourself.

Hired Help

I'll start with this: hired help is worth *every damn dollar* when it comes to getting yourself back some time and sanity. When I lived in NY, we were new homeowners, had just had twins, and were adjusting to the new financial life of having two new (and very expensive) dependents and a hefty mortgage over our heads. I couldn't justify hiring a housekeeper to help me clean the house, but I was also super anal about having an immaculate home. So, every week I did a deep dive clean, and by the time I was done, I felt proud and accomplished—for about five minutes. Then, those haters would come back and blow it all away. You know what haters I'm talking about:

- *Mom guilt for not spending time with my kids and cleaning instead*
- *Exhaustion because the only downtime I had that day was spent scrubbing my kitchen and bathroom*
- *Loneliness because I could have been at a playdate with my friend and her kid*
- *Resentment because my husband wasn't helping me clean the house*

The clean house couldn't compete with the awfulness I felt just minutes later that lingered and lingered and lingered. And, by the way, the house was a total shit show by the next day anyway. It was a vicious pattern of clean house, angry woman, dirty house, angry woman. Too many angry women for my taste, your taste, and probably every single person on this planet's taste.

When I moved to San Francisco, I knew my work schedule and commute would be more intense, and I knew I didn't want to sacrifice the little time I had at home with my family cleaning my house. Yet I wasn't about to live in a place that wasn't up to some pretty clean standards. So, I made it a non-negotiable to hire a cleaning crew every other week, and I never looked back. Investing in this service, as small and minuscule as it may seem, was a huge relief to my stress level and uplift to my mood. Did I think they cleaned as well as I did? No. Did I care enough to take back that load? Also no.

A big takeaway here is that when it comes to making a change like this, you have to commit. My commitment was to hire help and not feel bad about it. You need to be able to basically 'fix it and forget it'. I'm super analytical, so deciding on things like these hasn't always come easily to me. If you don't have the second portion of the commitment down, the rid of guilt, you won't be able to stick to it. Excuses will creep in one day when you have an extra hour of free time or get hit with an unexpected expense, and you'll cave back to your old ways of wanting to do-it-all.

I believe a lot of this stems deep from childhood. How many of you were raised with parents who 'did it all'? I think, especially if you have immigrant parents as I do, it's more normal than not to take on the home tasks, or really any tasks, alone. I don't know one woman in my family in Italy who pays someone to clean their house. I also don't know one woman in my family who works the hours I work while raising three small kids. It doesn't exist. So, get yourself the damn cleaning service and remember, you can't do it all. And you were never happy doing it all. So, don't do it all. Or you may lose it all. And by all, I mean your shit.

What else can you hire help for? The most beautiful part of living in the USA is that you can hire someone to do almost anything. Convenience should be a part of our national anthem. We're the founding fathers of the drive-thru, 24-hour pharmacies, Amazon prime, Task Rabbit, and basically any other convenient service you can think of. All you need to do is pay for it. So, decide what areas of your life you could benefit from outsourcing, schedule it in, and then forget it. Thank yourself later for gifting yourself the time and positivity that service has done to make your life that much better.

Coaches

I'm going to spend a few minutes delving into the fabulous world of life coaches. I guarantee for many of you reading this book when you hear the word life coach a skepticism may creep up inside you. I also guarantee that if you're one of these people, you've also never worked with a coach before, or at least not a good coach. Am I right or am I right? I know I'm right.

Coaches can bring even the most motivated overachiever to a level far higher than they ever even aspired to become. Coaches help you figure out ideas, gain clarity with those ideas, and then execute those ideas to your highest potential. Coaches are gods. If coaches formed a religious cult, I would strongly consider joining. That's how legit I think coaches are.

I've been fortunate to have had the incredible experience to work with three coaches over the years. Each was very different, and each helped me at very different points in my life. With each coaching experience, I gained insight, clarity, and made important life decisions. Without those coaching opportunities, I'm not sure I would have been able to do the same.

During my first coaching experience, I was at a crossroads. My career wasn't picking up financially, and neither was my husbands'. We had a substantial mortgage and a couple of kids, and every other expense that goes along with those things. It seemed like as soon as we took a step forward, we took two steps back—the washing machine broke or one of our kids needed a medical helmet. It was stressful, and we started questioning whether or not staying in the pricey suburbs of New

York, where we'd been born and raised, was really the right choice for the long term.

I let my coach know all of this. I told her, "I just want some financial cushion, not even to be able to buy anything in particular, but just to be able to go on a vacation or have some flexibility to make more memories with our kids." At the time, it seemed like every decision included a question about money. I remember leaving Costco and buying bare necessities while spending $300. "How do people do this?" I thought. The hard pill to swallow was that we both had pretty good jobs. How did all the bills add up so quickly?

My coach helped me realize a lot. She didn't give me advice. She didn't suggest a move or a career change or anything like that. She listened and asked the right questions so I would be motivated to take steps toward achieving what I wanted and needed at the time.

As I mentioned, we were greatly considering moving out of state to a more affordable part of the country. We even visited a couple of places to see if we could envision our lives there. My job security was important to me, and I needed to know I'd still have one if we decided to uproot ourselves to a state where neither one of us had a secure gig. Call it serendipitous or just fate, but a few months later, I was offered a substantial promotion, and after much thought and contemplation, we took a risk and moved ourselves cross country. That was life changing, to say the least.

My second experience with a coach was shortly after that move. I was settling into my new life and my new normal on the West Coast. I'd gone from working from home 75 percent of the time to commuting two hours daily. It was a huge transition, not to mention the increased workload, stress, and learning curve of starting a new role. On top of all that, my biggest priority, my family, was weighing on me. Was I taking good enough care of everyone? Was I still being a good mother? Was I present enough? Was I making any time for myself throughout all this?

Believe it or not, from those good conversations with my phenomenal coach, all based on my woes, I was able to develop the idea that eventually sparked my blog, this book, my business, and my mission. Years later, as I was clearing out the clutter in some stacks of papers, I came across my notes from one of those coaching sessions. My actionable steps at the time were focused on spending more time with my family and more time on myself. I wrote down: join a moms' group to make some friends, research working mom sites, start a blog. Years later, when I finally let the nagging entrepreneurial spirit in me back into my life, I contemplated varying ideas of businesses to start. I liked photography, should I do that? It seemed like the safest choice. My heart wasn't there though. My heart was still where my coach had helped me find it: serving the mom market through my voice, both written and spoken. I went for it…all because of that second coaching experience.

Finally, my most recent coaching experience got my ass back in gear to get this book done. If you ask most authors, they'll say that starting to write a book is not hard. It feels a lot like January 1st or 2nd or even 3rd when you're going to the gym daily, have your whole week meal prepped, and would probably pour dish soap on all the chocolate in your house because you're *that* connected to your goal of losing weight. Writing a book, in the beginning, is often easy. You have so many ideas. The words flow. The page numbers grow quickly. The content is a hot mess, but the thoughts, inspiration, and messages keep coming. It's like writing nirvana. Then, you get to a stage, maybe halfway through, when you start to lose some momentum. The words are more like teeth being pulled. The word count feels like it's going backwards. Does this even make sense anymore? Will anyone even want to read this? I have so many other things I need to do, like file my nails and count backward from 1000. I'm out. I think I'll watch Netflix tonight because the thought of opening my laptop right now is making me want to choose to fold all my kids' laundry into tiny squares ala Marie Kondo style rather than write any more content for my once passionate and sexy book. Much of this sad story is true, but, fortunately, has a happy ending. You're reading it, and it's because my coach put that spark back in me. My coach got rid of the doubt, the fear, the obstacles I didn't even realize I was facing and helped me realize that finishing this book and publishing it was going to be my reality. I'm so incredibly grateful I had that support to hold me accountable for getting my words on paper and hopefully inspiring others to take their dreams and do something with them too.

Working with a coach will help you figure out not only what you want, but an actionable way to get there. If you're an overachiever and want to wow yourself with even more than you thought was possible, get yourself a coach. But don't worry. If you don't get yourself a coach, you'll still do just fine here. The fact that you even decided to read this book and have made it this far shows me you're a badass mother who is so damn ready and able to momage the shit out of her time. So, keep reading. You're going places.

How to Ask for Help

Now that you've figured out all the untapped resources you have, you need to actually muster up the courage, the nerve, the (for lack of better word) *balls*, to ask for that help.

This is the hardest part.

As moms, we don't know how to lean on someone because we're always being leaned on. We have the weight of the world, or a comparably heavy sleeping toddler, on our shoulders and we know that one slight move may shake things up, waking that angelic babe up. It's exhausting to think about and a crazy way to live. Yet, most of us, if not all of us, are doing it—all day, every day.

Chances are when you think about asking for help, you fall into one of the following four categories:

1. You're worried about bothering the person you're asking for help.
2. You're anticipating you're not going to get the answer you want from the person you're asking.
3. You're feeling like a total loser asking for help because the world has painted a completely unrealistic picture of mothers *not* needing help.
4. You're unable to let someone else do a not-so-perfect job because, well, you already do it pretty damn perfect yourself.

Let's address, shall we?

1. You're worried about bothering the person you're asking for help.

If you're worried about bothering the person you're asking for help, let me start by asking you something. Would you feel bothered if your friend, sister, spouse, mother, fill-in-the-blank-person asked you for help? If you answered yes, then don't ask that person. If you answered no, then don't feel bad asking them. It's that simple.

I want to clue you in on an extensively researched piece of science that you may not know. Most people genuinely enjoy helping others. I mean, think about so many parts of your own life. What are things that stand out and make you feel good? How about teaching your kids to do something new, or better yet, helping them learn a new fact, soft skill, or life lesson? What about carrying an old lady's heavy bags to her car at the grocery store? Have you ever mentored someone at work? Or even paid it forward in the Starbucks drive-thru? These are all things that make you feel good about yourself and they're all about helping others. If you feel this surge of endorphins when you do something to help someone else, what makes you think the person helping you isn't going to feel the same? Don't you want to make people feel good? Then, let them help you. Period.

In case the people in your life are in the small percentage of humans who are ultra-narcissistic and could care less about anyone other than themselves, one of two things will happen. The person will still help you even though they really don't want to (you still win) or the person will (get ready for it) say no, which brings us to number two. Keep reading, mama. We're just getting started.

2. You're anticipating you're not going to get the answer you want from the person you're asking.

Let's start with this: Why are you being so negative? Haven't you ever heard of the self-fulfilling prophecy, *what you put out, you get back*. So, put out some positive vibes so you can get those good vibes right back, mama. If you envision negativity, you will likely get negativity. Make sense? Second, do you know what stops most people from doing things in life? I'll give you a hint. It's a four-letter word that starts with the letter F. Get your mind out of the gutter and stay with me, sister. Fear. F-E-A-R. Fear.

Fear is one of the biggest haters you will have to encounter in your life. She will make you question yourself. She will tell you-you're not good enough, not smart enough, not pretty enough, not worthy enough, just plain *not enough* and make you feel scared, intimidated, and undeserving. She's an awful neighbor next to your dream home. You need to know how to tune her *and* her bad music out.

I could write a-whole-nother book on this monster, but that's not where we're going to go with this. Bottom line: don't let fear stop you from doing *anything* in life, especially something as minuscule as asking for help. Let's move on.

3. You're feeling like a total loser asking for help because the world has painted a completely unrealistic picture of mothers *not* needing help.

If you're feeling like asking for help means you're failing at being a mom, you're not alone, and the world is to blame. Moms have always had the immense pressure to fulfill the roles of creators, nourishers, fixers, consolers, beauties, brains, etc. etc. etc. Now, we also wear the pants in many cases, if you know what I mean. We're bringing home the bacon, frying it up, and serving it with fine restaurant quality presentation. Then, we are cleaning the dishes and working off the calories to maintain our girlish figures. It's subhuman. It's exhausting. And most importantly, it's *not* sustainable.

I was out to brunch with my girlfriends one day, all of us moms. We all had babies within a year of each other. We all could relate to each and every story we told, emotions we were feeling, and problems we were facing at that moment. The empathy couldn't get any more real. We were all walking in each other's ballet flats day in and day out. During that conversation, we all offered to help each other out in a way that was so genuine, so comfortable, so downright honest, and true. "Just drop off the kids." "I don't mind at all-anytime." Yet, not one of us would end up taking the other up on that help…ever. Why? Because moms shouldn't need help. That's what this world has taught us to live by and brainwashed us to believe. It has corrupted our inner sense of vulnerability so much so that we end up sweeping it all up under the rug, along with the many Cheerios from today's snack.

As one of my favorite authors, Brené Brown, would say, "Vulnerability sounds like truth and feels like courage. Truth and courage aren't always comfortable, but they are never weakness."[3] The vulnerability here is the asking for help, the actual act of articulating that you need some support. It's

---

[3] Brené Brown, Daring Greatly: How the Courage to Be Vulnerable Transforms the Way We Live, Love, Parent, and Lead, (Penguin Group, 2012).

uncomfortable, but it's not a lack of strength. It's actually one of the bravest things you, as a mom, will ever do.

4. You're unable to let someone else do a not-so-perfect job because, well, you already do it pretty damn perfect yourself.

If you're unable to let someone else do a not-so-perfect job, the first step is admitting you have a problem: a control problem. I will start. My name is Marisa, and I have control issues. Do you? A lot of moms do. Think about it. It's almost inevitable in many cases. As a mom, you manage a lot of things. You're almost always in control. Yet, you also need help. Getting help means you relinquish some of that control. Oy vey- that's uncomfortable, isn't it? Yeah, it totally is.

Here's how you can work past your controlling habits without compromising your sanity. I mean, the purpose of time momagement is to get that balance and sanity back, not cause yourself severe anxiety. So, trust the process while playing your cards right with this one.

Ask yourself, "What are the things I could use help with?" List them all out, even the ones you think you'd never want help with at all, because-hey-you may change your mind someday. When you look at the list, there are certain items that may not make the cut because they're areas of your life you're extremely passionate about, or perhaps you've grown passionate about by default, simply because you handle them every day. Is it cleaning your house? Is it cooking dinners? Is it doing laundry? I mean, honestly, is anyone in their right mind passionate about doing laundry? If you are, then please open a dry cleaner or a laundromat, because the world needs more people like you to help the rest of us out.

If there are clear cut things you enjoy doing, want to maintain, and are non-negotiable when it comes to someone else being in control, cross them out. Breathe a sigh of relief and move on. If you've crossed everything out, start over and skip this step. You need to march to the beat of a different drum in this process. Next, the areas you're far less excited about doing, circle. These should be the areas that if someone else handled, with your incredibly detailed instructions, you'd be happy to relinquish. They'd give you back those hours to dedicate more mindfully to the things you are passionate about doing.

Lastly, determine how you can get someone else to perform those duties for you. A husband or partner, a kid, hired help, a service, the list goes on. Figure out which of those, even if it's just one, can be taken off your plate. Then, take it off and don't look back. Maybe those shirts won't be folded the way you like, or Wednesday dinners won't be as healthy as you would have preferred, but in the end, your mental health will thrive, and the once a week pizza shouldn't affect your weight negatively, that much.

The Communication Formula

If you're anything like me, in order to ask for help, you may need a communication formula. In my life, I like to have clear instructions on how to do things (I'm a *How's that Work* communicator), so formulas work for me. Because I also wrote this book, you are in so much luck, mama. I've developed a three-step process when it comes to asking for help that is sure to make you feel more confident, explain your request more clearly, and hopefully obtain the answer you're looking to get: a big, enthusiastic YES!

Here's what you're going to do: the **AYY Mami Method**: Ask, Why, You (AYY). The name is courtesy of my reggaetón lovin' days. Escuchame (listen up), mami:

A Is for the 'Ask'

When you're asking for help, clarify what you're asking for. Don't be vague; make it specific. What do you need? How much time will it take? What does it entail? Instead of saying, "I need help cleaning," say, "I need help washing the floors or putting the laundry away—or both." It needs to be clear or no one is going to get it, and then you are going to get frustrated and give up. You will start to think no one is capable of helping because no one does it like you, or no one wants to help—but this is often just because no one fully understands the request. Don't let that happen. Start with a clear, specific ask.

Y Is the 'whY'

Once you've laid out all the details of your ask, be sure to let the person know why you need that help. Do you feel like you are on the verge of a mental breakdown because you haven't laughed with your girlfriends in months? Is the disorder in your house making your head also feel disorganized and distressed? Do you just need an hour to soak in some sunshine without acting as a professional lifeguard, sunscreen applier, snack provider, or stomach sucker-inner? Lay it all out there. I know, this ain't easy. The why is often even more vulnerable than the ask. Be honest about it. The why makes you relatable. The why draws the connection. The why gets you the help from a place of empathy, compassion, and bonding.

Y Numero Dos Is the 'You'

Don't forget to tell the other person what's in it for them, even if it is just a more pleasant version of yourself to be around. Sometimes that is enough to seal the deal (I speak from personal experience with the hubs). Are you willing to swap some childcare with a friend? Are you planning to reciprocate the favor somehow? If you're hiring help, discuss the parameters of payment, relationship, and expectations from the start. And yes, a what's in it for them approach is important for anyone you're asking for help from. "I heard you clean Bonnie's house next door on Thursdays. Would you want to clean mine afterward, so you have back to back gigs where you don't need to sit in traffic driving elsewhere?"

Here's an example of the AYY Mami method in action:

Ask: *"Hey babe, can you watch the kids for two hours on Saturday afternoon, so I can get a mani-pedi? They have swim class during that window, so you just need to take them there. I'll pack the bag for you."*

whY: *"I haven't had the chance to do anything for me since my last haircut (two months ago), and I'm totally feeling cranky about my haggled mom-look these days. I know if I do something small like this I'll immediately feel better about myself."*

You: *"I'll happily reciprocate so you can watch the game with your friends on Sunday. Seriously-no guilt."*

Do you see how easy that was to implement? Three simple steps. My five-year-old could do this. Stop making excuses when it comes to asking for help and just AYY it, mami.

Let's Recap

- It takes a village. You can't do it all. Period.
- Think about who your tribe consists of. Can you recruit new members? Kids as young as two can manage age appropriate responsibilities at home.
- Excuses will try to get in the way of asking for help. Don't let those haters stop you from going where you need to go.
- Use the AYY Mami method next time you ask someone for help: Ask, whY, You.

Chapter 5

Sleep is for the Weak...and the Strong

"If I had a dollar for every night I got eight hours of sound sleep since becoming a mom; I'd be dead broke."
-Marisa Volpe Lonic

In this chapter, you'll learn:

- Why sleeping less doesn't equate to doing less.
- Why lack of sleep isn't the only reason you're tired.
- How to gain back an hour of sleep a day.

Sleep is such a hot commodity when you have kids. It's like the thing you look forward to the most at the end, beginning, and middle of, well, every day. Even moms who *'don't need that much sleep'* (not me, by the way) would probably give up their first-born child to take a 30-minute nap some days. Sleep is what you would choose if it were a choice between partying hard at a bar and making sweet love to your California King. Sleep. Always. Wins.

When I had the twins, I was a total zombie for the first month. Those 30 days felt a lot like the week between Christmas and New Year's. You don't know what day it is, ever. You're eating whatever is around and feeling ultra-fat. You're slightly blue, and you're realizing maybe you didn't accomplish all you wanted to that year (or that day if you're talking post-partum). Yet, you're also hopeful something will soon change with the coming of the new year (or next phase—the non-newborn one). This is kind of what that month was like, minus the sleep.

I often thought to myself, "If I could just get some sleep, I could handle all of this *like a boss*." The severe lack of sleep coupled with crazy post-partum hormones and new mom syndrome caused extreme anxiety, incredible self-doubt, and a total lack of confidence in my ability to not only perform simple parenting duties but to even just function as a normal human being.

The first night I was able to get five hours of straight, uninterrupted sleep, which by the way wasn't until those babes were *well* past the newborn phase, I felt like I'd just spent a week on vacation at a luxury resort. I probably cleaned my whole house or ran a marathon the next day. I can't really remember, but I'm sure it was something epic.

I could go on and on about how much a good night's sleep will make you feel, well, good. But, I won't. Because the reality of mom life is sleep will rarely be good and never be enough. And the outcome of that is, you either lay down and let lack of sleep win or, just like time, you make her your B, and you work with what you got...and, yes, also sneak in some extra zzz's here and there.

It's Not Only Lack of Sleep That's Making You Tired

When you really think about it, it's pretty incredible all the things you accomplish every day on the little sleep you often get as a mom. Here are some of the achievements you should already be patting yourself on the back for doing:

- Showering (sometimes this in itself is enough)
- Looking presentable (hair did, make-up on point, clean clothes that are fashionably acceptable for Target level standards)
- Getting to work on time (or really just getting to work)
- Running a meeting, hitting a deadline, or any other challenging work-related task
- Ensuring the growing humans in your household are eating enough (whether that's packing their lunch bags, cooking dinner, breastfeeding, bottle feeding or spoon-feeding them)

- Playing with your kids, teaching them something, reading to them, *all of this*
- Keeping your house non-hoarder status (maybe even clean by some folks' standards)
- Satisfying your man or partner
- And so much freaking more!

I mean, it is truly impressive when you think about it. Your body adjusts. Your energy level lifts. Your brain (yes, even your mom brain) creates more space for this added mental load even without having had the proper rest it needed the night, week, month, or even year before.

Chances are you're reading this right now, and I've slightly lost you because you're like, "Uh, no. Girl, I'm tired *all the time*. This ain't me." Stay with me, sister. I feel you. I've been there. But you know what, it's not just the lack of sleep that's making you tired. Here's how I figured this out.

I've had periods of my life, let's call them my twenties, where good and plentiful rest was a regular part of the gig. My twenties were filled with fun, food, and sleep. Lots of sleep. Sure, I worked hard. Sure, I had goals. Sure, I was busy. But none of that equated to any of the hard work, goals, and busyness I feel now as a mom. Yet, right now, I often have a higher amount of energy and accomplish way more in the less amount of non-used time I have. Here are some reasons why I *know* this is true:

I'm *way* more efficient: When I became a mom, I stopped spending time 'fucking around'. Now, I get shit done not because I want to, but because I have to. I've always been an uber-productive person, but even that drive to be productive sometimes doesn't hit its max unless there's a real 'have to,' like a deadline or a force bigger than you (ok smaller technically if you're talking about your baby). I'm not a fan of saying, "I don't have time for that." Yes, there's always time. But realistically, as a mom, you really don't have time to fuck around most of the time. You can't spend 35 minutes deciding where to eat because your tiny humans are going to melt down if you don't feed them stat. You can't relax on your couch watching Bravo in the middle of a Sunday afternoon because your TV permanently has PBS Kids on and, also, you have screen time rules. You don't fuck around...as much...anymore. You map out your errands to squeeze in as much as possible before nap time. You get 12 hours' worth of work done in eight so you can catch your train home and snuggle before bedtime. You fold laundry while listening to a podcast and ordering next month's diapers and wipes on Amazon. You are a multi-tasking queen whose 20-year old self's jaw would drop if she could see you now.

I eat healthier: Small step, big difference. In college, I weighed about 30 pounds more than I do now. Why? I ate more food that wasn't good for me. I also drank more alcohol than I do now, but we will leave that for my next point. Listen, I'm no health food nut. I eat In-n-Out Burger sometimes. I love dessert. And I will never say no to a piece of chocolate. I also, and I know this is going to sound so cliché so please don't judge, typically eat healthily and (wait for it) listen to my body. I know. I used to hear people say this and be like, "What does that even mean?!". Now I feel like I'm in the club, the 'listening to my body club.' It really does make a difference to eat because your body is craving something and not because of your emotions. Fill your emotional void with something other than food, and you will surely feel less tired.

I drink less: By drinking less, I mean less alcohol. Nowadays, a hangover at 6:00 a.m. with three small kids makes that night before buzz far less enticing. I mean, don't get me wrong, I wholeheartedly enjoy the relaxing side effects a glass of wine can have. I also like a good dirty Martini on special occasions. And pour me a glass of Bailey's on the rocks now and then and, I'm yours forever. But drinking and me only hang once in a blue moon these days. I've got far too much to do, as do you, to include indulging in drinks as frequently as I used to. I typically save my drinks for social events and *really shitty* days, both of which I have less often than I did before kids. Yep, believe it or not, I'm a much more tolerant, less agitated, and Zen person now that I have kids. Go figure. They've totally broken my wound up, hot-tempered, New York spirit. Or is that just the constant smell of pot here in California? Either way, I'm pretty calm, until I'm not. The aftermath of drinks isn't always worth the instant effect they provide for me. And less alcohol for me equates to more energy and less tiredness.

I take better care of myself: Besides the better diet and diminished binge drinking, I also take better care of myself on the whole. I'll share a small and almost meaningless example, but hear me out. I don't go to bed with make-up on. Isn't it just the worst feeling to wake up after sleeping with a full face of make-up? I feel like this happened to me almost every weekend when I was in my twenties, possibly related to some of that drinking that went on. Waking up with a clean face goes a long way. Other examples: I use really good skin and hair products. If you're feeling any sense of guilt for spending $64 on eye cream, ask yourself how many lattes you bought last month. My eye cream lasts about six months. When you break that down, it comes down to 35 cents a day or $2.45 a week. You can't even get a regular coffee (let alone a latte) for that price, and I know you're buying them more than one a month. I also do extra nice things for myself sometimes, like go to the spa. This isn't a frequent thing. I don't have a spa membership, although I kind of wish I did. But, I definitely treat my hard-working body a bit better now that I'm higher on the corporate ladder and can afford some of these luxuries.

I get better quality sleep: Quality not quantity. As you know, when we moved into our first real, adult home, we had just had the twins. We had a ton of expenses being new homeowners, renovating, and adding two dependents to our budget, but we didn't go cheap on buying our new mattress. Why? Because this is a place you spend (hopefully) a third of your day, and ultimately your life. Why would you not splurge a little? Also, we picked our mattress when I was eight months pregnant, so yeah, I went for the most comfortable thing in a very uncomfortable state. Money means nothing when your back hurts 24/7.

As you're likely experiencing, at this stage of mom life, time for sleep does not come easy. I am going to say this in the most non-scientific, yet factual way. I have no hard evidence to support it except reflecting on my own life and seeing every other sleep deprived mother I know out there. Here it is. Not only do sleep-deprived moms get shit done, but we also get *more* shit done with *far less* sleep than we ever have in our lives. I can't reference anything except the school of badass moms on that one. If you disagree, sue me. Or don't. Please don't. Maybe just send me an email and let me know so we can have an amicable discussion on it.

With that said, no matter how bad-ass we all are, we could all use a little more sleep now and then. And by now and then, I mean all the time. So, do you want to know how to fit more sleep into your time? There are five small steps you can start today that will guarantee to get you back an hour of sleep a day. A whole hour. If you don't feel like you need that hour to sleep, well—good for you, use it for something else. I, on the other hand, will go to sleep.

1. *Get off your phone.* Seriously, put it away. Don't look at just 'one quick thing' before you go to bed. I guarantee that one thing is going to turn into you scrolling and clicking for 45 minutes and before you know it, it's midnight, and you're exhausted.

2. *Bang out your to-dos in 30 minutes or less.* I've always been one who prefers to sleep in rather than go to bed early, so I'd rather prep all that I can the night before to keep snoozing in the am. I'm sure you have a daily or nightly list of tedious chores that have to get done. Power through them quickly. Do not deviate. Do not get distracted. Just get it done. Make a playlist of seven songs (which is about 30 minutes) and go. What used to take you much longer just earned you some added time for ZZZs.

3. *Stop binge watching.* Limit yourself to one episode. It will be there tomorrow. Close your eyes. Let it go.

4. *Aim for a set bedtime every day.* I know, semi-pathetic. You're a grown woman after all! Putting an alarm on your phone though to let you know it's time to hit the

sack will remind you (and hold you accountable) that it's time to get some rest.

5. *Make your sleep space Zen.* Make your bedroom a place you actually want to be in, relax in, sleep in. Do you need to invest in some new bedding without spit-up stains on it? Can you clear the clutter on your nightstand? What about some dryer sheets that smell like lavender, so your clean sheets smell heavenly? Having an inviting and clean space in your bedroom will draw you to this space and help you sleep easy.

One day I was hiking with a friend, and we were chatting about what we'd been up to. She'd just gotten back into the workforce after a six-month hiatus caring for her daughter and visiting her parents in France. Although this was far more interesting than what I'd been doing the past six months, I shared my latest. That's what friends are for, right? I told her I was knee deep in writing this book, and she replied by asking the question I often get in one way, shape, or form when people hear I carry the title of author in addition to the many others of wife, mother, executive, friend, etc. "When do you find the time to do it?" I told her that I was doing a lot of my writing at night, once the kids went to bed.

We continued our conversation. We delved into what I was covering in the book, and this chapter on sleep came up. She shared such wise words that I had to include them here. "Are you writing in bed?" she asked. "Yes," I replied. "It's the most comfortable place for me to write at that time of day." She responded firmly with, "Stop writing in bed," in her beautiful French accent. "Your bed is for two things: what you do with your husband and sleeping. That's it. Find a different place to write." I was so taken aback by these words, but in a good way. I had one of those, "Why didn't I think of that?" moments. It made so much sense. My bed should be a place of relaxation. My bed isn't the best or even right environment to spark creativity, energize my motivation, or fulfill my personal goals—unless you count having a baby (sorry, I had to).

From then on, I made the conscious decision to *not* "work" in my bed, even on my passionate projects. I created a designated space where I'd write on the regular each night and what I found was that the separation of church and state (writing and sleep) helped me get to sleep more quickly and sleep more deeply. I'd encourage you to do the same. Stop checking emails in bed, or even watching TV in bed if you can help it (to be honest, this one I still do-I'm human). Basically, make your bed your sleep sanctuary so you get the best sleep you can. I know it's not hard when you're utterly exhausted to comprehend that. I bet you feel like any sleep will do. Why not try it? What do you have to lose? Clearly not sleep.

Besides the long period of sleeplessness that having young kids brings, there are also smaller intervals of time where even more time is taken away from my hours of sleep. For example, when I have an important project I'm working on with a deadline, I may need to dedicate more time to this and some of that time needs to be stolen from Peter (sleep) to be given to Paul (project). The important reminder here, especially for someone like me who really loves her sleep, is that these periods are temporary. Besides that, if I'm going to spend a bunch more hours finishing this book or creating that marketing campaign or researching our family vacation, it's because I'm going to get some intrinsic and hopefully extrinsic payoff. I know if I put the work in now, the outcome is going to be great. I'm ok with that.

If you are too, then you'll keep going. If you're not, then you'll fall asleep.

The takeaway here? Sleep all the hours you can, but don't ever let being tired stop you from doing something you want to do, because realistically, you're still doing everything else for everyone else with that little sleep now. It is totally possible to do all the things with all the sleep. It is also totally possible to do all the things with far less sleep. When you really want to do something, you'll do it. Being tired won't be an excuse. You'll power through and get it done. Why? Because you're a mother. You do it every day. Why not start doing the same thing for yourself?

Let's Recap

- Write down all the shit you're doing every day despite not having enough sleep. Then look at your list and say, "Damn girl, you the shit."
- Take good care of yourself. Eat better. Drink less. Buy some good face cream.
- Focus on ways to get back an hour of sleep per day like not checking your phone before bed and setting a bedtime alarm on your phone.
- Don't ever let being tired stop you from doing what you want to do.
- But also, take a nap if you need one.

Chapter 6

Repeat

"Motivation gets you started. Habit keeps you going."
-Jim Rohn

In this chapter, you'll learn:

- What it takes to form a habit.
- How to get back on the bandwagon when you fall off.
- Why planning ahead is a necessity for creating a lifestyle.
- How to hold yourself accountable to keep at it.

Think back to when you were learning to tie your shoes (if you can remember), or drive a car, or even how to use Microsoft Excel. The common denominator all these milestones have is this: the more you performed these actions, the better you got.

Have you ever been on a kick-ass gym routine? Or started eating healthier? Or even stopped doing something, like biting your nails? I bet the beginning was hard. Maybe it even sucked. You were probably sore from the gym, had sugar cravings worse than weird preggo ones, or smacked your hand away from your mouth like 30 times a day. After a few days, it got slightly easier. After a few weeks, you could hardly remember what life was like before this lifestyle change.

As I mentioned earlier in this book, it's a proven fact that it takes 21 days to form a new habit. Twenty-one days. It's not easy. Most people don't actually follow through. They fall off the bandwagon. It's human nature. But you already know, mama, you are subhuman. You've literally grown a person in your body, pushed them out (or had them extracted via gruesome surgery), then maybe even produced all that person's food while recovering from the trauma your body and mind just endured. If you adopted, you went through the emotional upheaval most people are incapable of handling, for a person you'd never even met, but already knew you loved. And now, you juggle all the things, and I bet you still find it within yourself to smile, be grateful, and live a life of positivity despite some days where the odds feel against you.

You make the impossible possible. Does 21 days of forming a new habit really intimidate you? The secret sauce to making any of your intended time momagement techniques stick in your daily life is simple: First, repeat. Do that shit over and over again. Second, start with one small habit or change at a time. The easier this habit is to add to your daily life, the more likely you are to actually continue doing it. Third and lastly, you need to give yourself some love, and by love, I mean tough love. Hold yourself accountable. Get it done. You need to be your own cheerleader in a police uniform, cheering yourself on and celebrating your victories while also making yourself obey the law. Sometimes you'll need to let yourself go with just a warning, but most times, you're going to remind yourself of the high-priced ticket (or in this case, the consequence) of not following through on your new habit. Don't worry. I've got tips on how you actually do it. I mean, I am an expert time momager after all.

In 2010, I decided I wanted to train for a half marathon. I was a newlywed, and after I'd spent a bunch of time and effort getting ultra-fit for my wedding, I took a much-needed break from food deprivation and insane workouts. I was also now living with my new husband full time, who loved and still does love, to eat. He's a total freak of nature. He eats anything and everything, in portions large enough to feed a family of four, and never gains a pound. For years, when I point out he should eat healthier or work out, he just laughs and says, "You're so jealous." And honestly, I kind of am! What the hell?!

Back to the story though, the most I'd ever run was three miles, and that was probably less than five times in my entire lifetime. To be real, I didn't even really like running. What I *did* like was being fit, and I needed a goal to get me back on a healthy track if I was going to be spending my life with this skinny heifer, my husband. Besides that, the idea of being able to accomplish something like running a half marathon was super captivating to me.

I had to make it a habit to run on the regular. I started with a training plan that I found online and then slightly modified it to fit my life. There were three runs a week that were "short" and would gradually become "less short," but were still categorized as "short." To this day, I don't think six miles is a short run, but whatever. Then, there was a long distance run each week, which I'd do on the weekends, that would increasingly become longer and longer until the final week of training when I basically ran the whole half marathon.

Soon enough, running became habitual for me. I spent the next four months running four days a week, steadily increasing my distance and throwing in a long, incredulous run I never thought I'd make it through on the weekends.

I did this all through the brutal winter weather of New York. I ran on the treadmill after work and came home a sweaty, hot mess on the train afterward because I knew I'd never have the motivation if I went after the commute. I ran through frigid temperatures on weekend mornings because if I waited for the afternoon hours, excuses would be more likely to get the best of me.

By the time May 1st hit, I was in awe of what I had been able to do. The feeling of running those 13.1 miles was unbelievable. I've never been an incredibly athletic person. I've never considered myself "a runner," yet, here I was crossing the finish line with thousands of other runners.

The Four-Letter Word That Makes It All Happen

What got me across that finish line was forming a habit: repeating by making the time to make it happen, starting with one small change (or short run) at a time, and being my own worst enemy and biggest fan at the same time. That's it.

So how do you ensure you'll rinse and repeat? How can you prevent yourself from falling off the bandwagon? Or if you do fall (hey, it happens), how do you get back up and keep going? One word, mama. The word that has gotten me so far in life. The word that has made me unbearable to some and admirable to others. The four-letter word that gives me chills, makes me happy, excites me, and invigorates me. Here it is:

PLAN.
Plan it.
Plan ahead.
Have a plan A, plan B, plan C, and plan D.
Make plans.
Schedule plans.
Re-schedule plans if you have to cancel plans.
Plan, plan, plan.

In my mom life, as is likely the case in yours, without a plan, it rarely gets done. I don't know about you, but dinner doesn't make itself unless I plan it in advance. Unless you're married to one of those amazing guys who takes it upon himself to make a delicious, healthy dinner with all the food groups, using food you already have in your fridge, you need to plan. In my house, dinner ain't happening unless I've given it some thought in advance, or texted my husband very explicit instructions regarding oven temperature, cook time, and the ratio of olive oil to vinegar. Otherwise, it's most likely takeout, which does sometimes happen—even on my watch. I'm human.

What else needs planning? Family vacations don't typically happen unless they're planned in advance, right? You've got to book an Airbnb with enough space for your whole crew and hopefully more than one bedroom, so you can actually have a space away from the little people. You need to book your flights, hopefully not during the time of day of your kids' routine meltdown. You probably have to save for that trip because damn girl, Disney is expensive!

Planning is just part of the mom job. And it is a *big* part of the job. And to some extent, you are doing a lot of this already. But, maybe, just maybe, you want to be a better planner, a *BP*. You're probably a damn good planner for everyone else, but planning for you might not be your strong point.

The thing to remember when it comes to planning, even for the BPs in this world, is not to overdo it. You know, like when you plan to start your week off on Monday with a bang. You plan to drink a protein shake for breakfast, workout hardcore, eat a salad with no dressing for lunch, and drink your coffee black. Let's say you typically already do all of these things each week, except you normally put half-and-half in your coffee. Because the rest of the things are already a part of your routine, your Monday may turn out just fine because you are only making one change: not adding half-and-half to your coffee. If you continued this for 21-days, you'd turn into a badass black coffee drinker, and all would be fine in the world.

What I actually think, though, is that your life before this Monday consisted of a Starbucks latte and croissant for breakfast, power walking from your car to the preschool drop off, that is only 20 steps away, and eating a burrito for lunch. If that's the case, your Monday diet motivation will likely be pretty depleted by Thursday. Making so many changes to your daily habits at one time doesn't typically work out well for the long term. Those 21 days are going to feel like 21 years. No matter how many dressing-less salads you meal prep or protein shakes you down, there will most likely be lots of slip-ups along the way. The slip-ups will lead to frustration, which will likely lead to defeat.

You need to plan accordingly. Plan to change one habit at a time. Once that habit starts to feel, well, habitual (like something you do with little to no effort because it's a normal part of your routine), then plan in your next layer.

When to Bend so You Don't Break

Now, I've always been a planner. I'm a little Type A, and this is just part of my DNA. It's typically worked well for me. It's helped me achieve some amazing things. It's helped me get places. It's helped me make big investments. I'm not complaining. But planning can be a blessing and a curse. You've got to know when to stick to the plan and when just to let it go. Being flexible when it comes to planning is crucial, or else your plan is not going to help you, it's going to break you.

Let's take an example that solidifies what I just said about knowing when to bend, so you don't break. This is something that happens to me pretty frequently. How often are you late? I feel like lateness has become a pretty regular occurrence in my life. I like to blame something or someone other than myself, even though I know I'm responsible for my own actions. For this particular example, 90 percent of the time, it's really not my fault. It's all my kids. I'm guessing the same goes for you. Do you know how I know? It's basically a proven fact that kids make you late. Kids make you late, even when you start getting ready for a 10:00 a.m. event at 6:00 a.m. Kids are going to make you late. You can plan all you want, have seven back-up plans, and do everything right, but those kids are still going to make you late. My kids have taught me that no matter how much of an MBA of a planner you are, they're still going to shit all over it (sometimes that literally means shit all over it—yes, it's happened to me). But in the end, it all works out.

I want you to take some words of wisdom from this example. Plan all you want. Try your best to stick to that plan. And when shit happens (no pun intended), be ready to take a deep breath and try again. A slight deviation from the plan doesn't mean you should give up and throw it all away. It means you deviate and plan again. Because that's what BPs do. They learn, they accept, and they keep going—late and all.

Now, what if the plan is going just fine and we're the culprits? We're the ones who deviate intentionally from the plan? Yeah, this happens. Think about the last time you abruptly stopped working toward something. Maybe it was your diet, or your workout routine, or even your commitment to cooking dinner or reading a book. It can happen with anything you intend to do. Sometimes even us planners, with all good intentions, don't follow the yellow brick road all the way to the habit-forming end. We stray away. We find excuses. We give up. Have you been there? I have.

As mentioned, in college, I was about 30 pounds heavier than I weigh now. I'd formed some pretty bad habits when it came to eating. I exercised, a lot—way more than I do now. In fact, I even taught exercise classes, if you can believe it. Yes! I was an AFAA certified instructor, teaching anything from step aerobics to cardio kickboxing. But I still didn't feel good in my own skin. It was because I couldn't kick the unhealthy habits I'd developed. I'd tried so many diets and I would almost always wander off that yellow brick diet road before the 21 days were up. I'd lose five pounds and gain 10. It was a totally self-sabotaging lifestyle. I'd be super pumped about a new diet, buy all the protein powder to make the shakes or fresh fruits and veggies to detox. I would have so much motivation for a few days, and then fail miserably, and end up feeling worse than before I'd started. I couldn't form a healthy habit.

It wasn't until I permanently left college life and moved back in with my parents (yikes) that I finally got back to the real me, a real me who I'd never really even known. I mean, I was basically still a growing teenager when I'd left for school. Now, I was a twenty-something-year-old woman with a Master's Degree, working out on the regular, eating much healthier, and drinking a hell of a lot less tequila. Those pounds melted off. Within a year, I'd shed all 30 of them and was comfortable in my own skin.

The reason this change was able to happen so "easily" (I say easily with sarcasm because losing weight is never really easy or effortless, but I want to show you the difference in how I actually made this happen without the constant failures I'd experienced in the past), is because I had made some drastic changes to my environment. The bad habits I'd formed in college weren't as haunting because I wasn't surrounded by the same schedule, people, work, and living environment. Typically, big changes like this trigger major opportunities to form new habits (either good or bad). Living back at home with my parents, I could easily get back into the habit of eating healthier because I lived with my Italian chef father who cooked homemade, healthy meals daily. I could practice healthier sleep and social patterns because I was now adulting: working full time, dating someone seriously, and saving for my first home.

The reason I tell you this story is because without forming a legit habit of making time for *you* and filling it with what *you* want to do with it, you will enter into the vicious cycle I experienced with my weight. Making time for you needs to be a regular occurrence, a routine, a must-do. If it's not, here's what you might experience.

Me-time → Work, work, work, work, work → Resentment, Anger, Guilt → Lashing Out at Everyone → Slight Mental Breakdown → Back to Me-time

Don't wait for that slight mental breakdown. Don't ruin your relationship. Don't yell at your kids. Don't feel bad for yourself, or worse yet, feel guilty. Don't push yourself to a breaking point of working so hard that you are basically ready to fall over if one more person asks you for something. Schedule yourself into your life. It sounds so silly, but that simple step of writing down that time on your calendar or entering it into your phone holds you accountable. Most times, when you don't schedule it, you don't do it.

Then, even on a week when you feel like deviating for whatever reason, which is usually just a made-up excuse in that mom-guilt brain of yours, still do it. I know this sounds much easier said than done. I know those "reasons," aka excuses, sound legit. They are so damn persuasive, convincing, charismatic, and tempting. Don't forget; they're also haters. They don't want you to succeed. They don't want you to be better, and especially not better than them. But you *are* better. So, tell them to back off. And just do it.

I once saw a quote that I think really resonates here: "Do something today your future self will thank you for." When your phone notifications are going off from social media likes, but you've scheduled yourself for a 30-minute work-out, which option do you think your future self will feel the most value from an hour later? Will you feel your best self after you've scrolled through random people's fake lives or after you've got endorphins pumping through your body? Will you feel better after you've blow dried your hair or if you've let your hair airdry into a frizzy hot mess and watched that Netflix show? Pick the one that makes your future self a happy self. Always. Or at least pick it nine times out of 10.

Let's Recap

- The secret sauce to forming a habit is repeating, taking one small step at a time, and holding yourself accountable.
- If you want to stay on the bandwagon, planning is crucial.
- Do something your future self will thank you for. Think about how you'll feel in an hour if you stick to your plan and let that guide your next step.

Chapter 7

How Momagement and Minimalism Mingle

"I'd rather have extra space and extra time than extra stuff."
-Francine Jay

In this chapter, you'll learn:

- Why momagement can't live without minimalism.
- Ways to live a minimalist life without necessarily getting rid of all your stuff.
- Why having a minimalist mindset is a necessity for living a more positive and plentiful life.

119

If Momagement had a BFF, her name would be Minimalism. It's hard to have one without the other. To be really good at momaging your time, you need to start with some real mindfulness geared toward living a more minimalist life. I'm a work in progress, myself, as I consider myself a semi-minimalist mama. I like to shop. I like to do a lot. I like to achieve a lot. I've also figured out how to scale back, buy what I need, do enough, achieve the bigger picture goals, and basically live my best life. And who doesn't want to be living their best life?

Becoming more mindful of how much stuff you own and how much time you have is like being able to inhale through your nose and taste delicious food after an awful cold. It feels so good. You can sleep with your mouth closed. You can taste those calories. You can live again. It's like rounding the corner of your second trimester when your morning sickness suddenly dissipates, your bump doesn't look like you just ate too many tacos, and you no longer have narcoleptic episodes at awkward times, like that meeting with your company's board of directors. You're able to focus on the awesome parts of being pregnant, like rocking cute maternity clothes, the 20-week sonogram, gender reveal, and choosing a name for your new addition.

Having a minimalist mindset lets you focus on the important things. And yes, those cute maternity clothes are important! Having a minimalist mindset keeps you engaged in the good and rids your life of the bad. Having a minimalist mindset guides you in the direction you're meant to go. Yes, there may be traffic. Yes, there may be detours. But minimalism will still get you there while making that road trip an enjoyable ride fully equipped with your favorite songs, the best snacks, and beautiful sites to see along the way.

Personally, I think there's always room for improvement when you're striving for minimalism. And I'm not a drastic example myself. Case in point: I own seven pairs of jeans and only wear jeans two to three times per week. Why, then, do I need seven pairs of jeans? Spoiler alert—I don't have the answer. What I do believe, though, is that simply shifting the way you look at things, looking at them through a minimalist pair of lenses, can really help transform your ability to feel more fulfilled with a lot less stuff cluttering up your home, your mind, your calendar, and your life in general.

Since becoming a mom, I've moved homes four times. Moving is a good excuse and a catalyst, in my honest opinion, for becoming more of a minimalist. It forces you to purge. It motivates you to organize. It opens your eyes to what's necessary and what's not.

I try to live a minimalist mom life, but I'm not hardcore. I have way too many black shirts. I have an entire set of wedding china I've never used in my life. And I still really enjoy shopping. Ever hear the term 'retail therapy?" Spending two hours in a TJ Maxx is the equivalent of going to *the best* therapist for me. I feel equally satisfied and rejuvenated after both experiences.

Being mindful of the amount of stuff (and time) you have, though, is *really* important. And often, having less equates to feeling more complete, more balanced, and more sane.

At the start of 2019, Netflix released the mini-series "Tidying Up with Marie Kondo". I'd heard of Marie before, but never read her book or adapted her lifestyle. I'm already semi-minimalist, I thought. I'm good. I resisted the urge to watch the show because I had other priorities, writing this book for one. I didn't want to dedicate those hours of my time to a show, even one that everyone was raving about, and I'm pretty sure The Container Store stocks were through the roof over. After many nights of writing and reading and writing some more, I gave myself a 'mental break' and watched the first episode. Wow.

I filled a couple of ThredUp bags. I went through the final two yet-to-be-unpacked boxes full of paper and books that had been sitting in my closet since we'd moved six months prior. I even convinced my husband to build me a desk in my closet to give me the proper workspace I'd been missing since we'd been in our new home. I was on minimalism/organization fire.

The whole experience was extremely gratifying, but it also helped me adopt another level of minimalism. When I looked at my drawer of perfectly folded black squares of shirts, it made me think twice about buying another. When I saw the joy donating toys my kids didn't play with anymore brought to a family friend, my heart felt fuller. It was a domino effect on many, many areas of my life.

You might be asking, how does Marie Kondo'ing my life relate to my time? Here's how. When your life is in order, your mind is in order. When your mind is in order, you think more clearly, react less emotionally, and function more peacefully. When you let all that stuff in your life build up and become an overwhelming mess, it's really hard to muster up the energy to tackle it.

The thing about having space, both mentally and physically, is that you feel free. You're able to do what you want when you want because you're unrestricted. Let's exemplify this. Having a lot of stuff often means spending a lot of money, which often means not being able to spend that money elsewhere in other areas of your life, like experiences with your family, travel, or self-care. By buying less stuff, you give yourself more financial freedom to spend your funds in areas that potentially fit with your time momagement goals. You will also feel an internal satisfaction sometimes if you just save that money instead of buying something with it. I don't know about you, but any time I've been able to save a significant amount of money, the mere act of looking at my bank account feels so damn good.

Busy Doesn't Mean Productive

Having a busy schedule often doesn't mean having a productive one. Tim Ferris, New York Times best-selling author of many amazing books including *The 4-Hour Workweek*, says, "Focus on being productive, not being busy."[4] Learning when to say, "No" is equally as important as knowing when to say, "Yes." Say, "Yes" to things that help you get closer to and give you energy or minutes toward your time momagement goals, even if it is an indirect route there. Say, "No" to things that aren't necessary in your life and aren't bringing you any closer to your time momagement goals. Many of your "No's" will end up including your haters when you really start to think about what and who they are.

---

[4] Timothy Feriss , *The 4-Hour Workweek*, (New York, Harmony Books, 2009)

Having a mental load heavier than your tantruming toddler is like being over accessorized. You love all your jewelry, but you would never wear it all at once. Know what to pick and choose and what will sit in your jewelry box until you're wearing the perfect outfit that requires its presence. Some days, I choose a chunky necklace or vibrant earrings. Most days, I'm a simple studs, watch, and wedding ring type of gal.

This minimalist life wasn't always the case with me. I've learned to compartmentalize what I have to do and eat away at it one bite at a time, rather than feeling the overwhelm and stress most moms feel. Your everyday should be a maintainable way of life. If it's not, you need to change it. Marie Forleo, bestselling author and creator of B-School, says, "Overwhelm is a choice."[5] And she's absolutely right.

When I was growing up in Italy, I noticed just how minimalist other cultures were compared to the American way of life. My friends in Italy dressed beautifully, in designer clothes even. They always looked impeccable. Yet, they also had much fewer things and lived in much smaller spaces than we do. Yes, even smaller than those of us living in/near major cities where real estate is extremely expensive, and our homes are pretty small. Most even earned much less than we do, so the spending, by default, had to be less.

The difference between how my Italian friends lived and how my American friends lived was this: the Italians purchased one thing vs. the Americans purchased nine. They owned one Armani black top vs. seven H&M, Old Navy, and Gap black tops. They had one amazingly cool pair of jeans that they wore

---

[5] Marie Forleo, www.marieforleo.com

repeatedly and styled differently. As I mentioned, I own seven pairs of jeans. This is a huge scale back from where I used to be, by the way. There's still work to be done here, but for now, I'm semi-minimalist, and that's good enough for me.

Marie Kondo says to only keep things that spark joy in your life. You could take this to the extreme and decide that your toaster or your thermometer or your kitchen table doesn't spark joy for you. Maybe they don't, but sometimes you need these essentials to make your life function. When I can't just get rid of something in my life that doesn't spark joy, I think about how I can change it. For example, the home we moved into in 2018 had a very different look and feel than any previous homes we'd lived in. Our furniture, consequently, didn't work. Most of it, actually, really clashed. Our dining room table, a big investment piece we'd purchased just four years prior, was a piece we couldn't live without, yet it wasn't sparking joy for me in my new space. It just didn't fit.

Now, I'm a practical person. While I thought about buying a new table, there were so many other necessary items we needed in our home. There were other things that took priority when I thought about where our finances were going to go toward home improvements. Besides that, I have three little kids. I wasn't sure this was the best time in our kid raising timeline to invest in a new table, especially one where they did their daily artwork and crafts on.

When you want something, you need to figure out what the best solution is that will work with all areas of your life. If I wanted a new table, what did that mean? Would I have to figure out a way to make more money to justify a big purchase? That's not how I wanted to be spending my time. It wasn't worth it to me. Negotiating what you do with your time is your choice, as you know. You're the best person to make those wholehearted, big picture decisions, even for something as trivial as buying a new dining room table.

I decided I was going to paint the legs of the table from a cream color to black and distress them to match more of the grey tones our new house had throughout. The investment of a $15 quart of paint and three evenings of painting and sanding made me feel good about my decision to not just add stuff, but to work with what I had. Adding a new table meant adding more financial stress, arguments with my husband about which table to purchase, and being hyper-protective of a nice, new piece of furniture around three active boys! Working with what I had already was the right, minimalist solution for now.

You can apply this concept to so many areas of your life. Just like those social media Instamom influencers whose kids are wearing the coolest outfits in all their pictures, you need to remember that a cool outfit every day when you're two means shit to that two-year-old. They don't care. They're still going to throw up all over it, spill stuff all over it, color all over it, and outgrow it in five minutes. Buy a couple of gorgeous outfits, take your memory lasting photos and the rest of the days, dress them in the same four, stained things over and over again. Stop sacrificing your time on things and everything that goes along with those things and start using it in more meaningful ways. Less truly is more when it comes to time momagement.

Let's Recap

- You can't be a good time momager without having a minimalist mindset.
- Less stuff = more time.
- When your house is in order, so are you. Now go purge.

Chapter 8

Look Ahead and Behind, Not Side to Side

"Want to know how to make yourself instantly unhappy? Compare yourself with someone else."

-Fumio Sasaki

In this chapter, you'll learn:

- Why you shouldn't compare yourself to everyone and everything you see on social media.
- How past experiences can help shape the way you momage your time.
- How daily presence and mindset are simple ways to improve how you're spending your time.

129

It's easy to let past decisions, people, and even past time momagement habits pressure you into feeling like you can't possibly live a different future. The questionable influence isn't limited to your own self either. That doubt plays a key role when you compare yourself to other peeps out there.

I could never work out daily like Diana does. She has a full-time nanny and makes a ton more money than I do.

I wouldn't be able to start a company baking desserts. My kitchen isn't big enough like Claire's is.

I couldn't possibly figure that out. Elle's got an MBA and is way smarter than me.

As a mom, it's pretty common to feel like you're anything but perfect, especially when you see all the fake social media moms posting incredible photos of themselves and their kids. I will raise my hand (hell, I will raise both hands) with you, mama if someone asks if I've done this self-shaming before. I absolutely have. It's not only a total time suck. It's a total ego kick, guilt boost, and self-doubt infuser. And now that we've bonded over our social media rabbit hole frenzies, I have two words for you: Photoshop and Filters. We all know your secrets, Instamombeauties because we also use them. I digress. My point is this. You have no freaking idea what is happening over on the other side of that DM. That woman could be going through an awful divorce. Those kids could be battling emotional issues or struggling with learning disabilities. Remember, the grass isn't always greener. They used a filter.

Being a time momager means you own your time and any obstacle that could potentially be a block in the road from making it yours. Your time is your journey because your time makes up your life. Why wouldn't you want that life to be the one you've always dreamed it would be? It starts with your time. Stop letting mindless shit get in the way of how you're spending your time and the way your dream life should look. You *can* be in control of it, so *take* control of it. And when you feel like you've lost control (and you will sometimes), don't surrender. Just take a deep breath, a nap, or even a step back and reboot yourself back to being that controlling self you were meant to be, mama.

In 2008, I got this idea about starting a baby/kids clothing line with international phrases written on the clothes. It wasn't until 2012 that I actually launched it. Yes, it took me four years to bring this idea to fruition. During that time, there were tons of setbacks. For starters, I knew nothing about the clothing industry, yet alone the kids clothing industry. I didn't know how I'd even get these designs on the clothes themselves. And, by the way, what designs? All I had was an idea and some translated cutesy phrases I envisioned being on adorable onesies. Basically, I had a dream. And that was all I had.

I could have quit 100 times. I could have abandoned this dream. But, since I already gave you the spoiler alert above, you know I didn't. Here's what I did instead:

I knew zero about getting designs on clothing, so I took a screen-printing class.

I owned nothing to actually execute the process, so I purchased screen printing equipment.

I learned (a small part) of Photoshop and designed the prints.

I had no actual clothes to print on, so I researched kids' blank clothing articles and got some inventory.

I had nowhere to sell my inventory, so I made a website.

I knew I needed to become a legit business, so I became an LLC.

I made a ton of mistakes and ruined a lot of expensive organic onesies, but I printed the clothes and finally got some that were sellable.

I figured cute kids wearing the clothes would help my marketing, so I set up a photoshoot with my friends' kids.

I marketed the clothes on social media, at mom events, baby showers, you name it.

I sold a bunch of clothes.

Do you see a reoccurring theme here? I. *I* did it. *I* learned it. *I* figured it out. *I* executed. At the time, I also didn't have kids, but I was working full-time. All of my downtime was spent creating this business. And the satisfaction that came from launching that dream was unbelievably satisfying.

Now, this business didn't thrive and ultimately didn't make it. But, it was also such a sweet and empowering step in my life.

Because I did it all without asking for enough support, when life threw me some intense curve balls, I couldn't sustain it solo. In early 2013, I got pregnant...with twins...both surprises, one more than the other. I couldn't mentally withstand running a business I was still learning daily how to do, working a full-time job, purchasing our first home, being a high-risk, first-time pregnant mama, and preparing for twin motherhood. I let the business fizzle.

I didn't feel like a failure...most days. In the end, I had accomplished what I didn't even know I'd wanted. I'd done all the things I didn't think I could do. And that turned out to be enough for that particular milestone. My needs changed. My passions changed. And I was ok with it.

If I hadn't felt that sense of peace, I would have kept going. I would have given that business every single piece of me. I would have (hopefully) learned to delegate more. But in the end, I didn't do any of that, and my business ultimately failed. Yet, I took something away from it. Many things actually.

These past "mistakes," or what I would rather call "experiences," help us make better decisions in the future when it comes not only to managing our time but prioritizing the things that matter. For me, the process of starting that business and ultimately watching it fail are huge wins and lessons I carry with me. Did it suck when people asked me how my business was doing, and I would answer, "Oh yeah, that...?" Kind of. It wasn't the way I'd wanted it to go, but I take full ownership of why it went the way it did and have no regrets. Now I know I can basically figure anything out. I know if I'd really wanted to find a way to make that business survive, I would have. I would have changed my designs, or my color schemes, or my price point if it meant keeping sales moving. I would have outsourced more support if things grew to the point where I wasn't able to keep up. I wouldn't have let the business slip through my fingers if it was the direction I was meant and called to go. I would have made it my top priority, or at least one of my top priorities because when you compare a new business with new twins, the twins will always win.

These experiences don't always need to be our own experiences where we were the main decision-makers. They could be how we were raised or something we observed a friend or relative doing. For example, growing up, my parents worked unconventional schedules. My dad was a chef and was rarely around on the weekends. My mom was exhausted by Sunday because she'd spend all week working, caring for me solo in the evenings, and then all-day Saturday cleaning our house. Our house was always immaculate, and I owe my semi OCD cleaning skills to that sparkly clean woman.

Nonetheless, Sundays, consequently, were typically a quiet day. They were low key. I could even reference them, in my case, as 'slightly blue." The chores were done. The sheets were clean. The floor was spotless. The vibe was a restful one. My mom might even nap. I'm sure, as a mom, the canvas I've just painted of a clean, quiet house and a day of rest sounds like an incredible feat you'd pay good money to experience. As a child though, and especially being an only child for a good portion of my early years, it was sort of boring. Pair that with the worrier I was and the school week looming ahead, and I caught the Sunday blues.

When I was in high school, I remember being in the driver's ed car with our eclectic teacher. Now, when you think about someone who chooses the career of driver's ed teacher for a living, it seems inevitable that this person might be pretty damn interesting, or potentially a bit of a weirdo. My driver's ed teacher was both. He was in a band, was obsessed with the color purple (his purple car had a purple tail on it—no joke), and often had some really deep thoughts to share with three random high school kids from different social groups alphabetically placed together in the *purple people eater*. I wouldn't be able to tell you his name because for some reason all the other fun facts about this man stayed with me—except for the one important, small detail of his name. I will, however, always remember what he said about the Sunday blues. He spoke about it in such a matter of fact sort of way, like a doctor telling you you have strep throat. "Oh yeah, the Sunday blues," he said. "That will stay with you forever."

What?! How could the owner of a 1992 purple vehicle know what the Sunday blues were and that it would be an anxious driven, depression-inducing, sad, sad part of my life...*forever*? At the time, my high school self-thought, "Well, damn. I guess that's the end of a normal life for me."

As I got older and gained more and more control of my time, my schedule, and my life, I realized that what Mr. Driver's Ed teacher had said was total bullshit. I could kick the Sunday blues out of my life if I wanted to. I could make sure the Sunday blues weren't a part of me anymore. And I did.

Now, I make a conscious effort to ensure my household's Sunday vibes are far different than those I felt growing up. This isn't a martyr moment or a mess up on my parents' end. The circumstances were different. Unconventional schedules, one child, finances, generations, all of it. Also, in her defense, as a kid, I never told my mom I hated Sundays or felt blue about them. I'm sure if I had, she would have made some sort of change because that's the kind of mom she was and still is. I get a lot of my drive and perseverance from her. Growing up with the Sunday blues was a learning lesson of how I wanted to momage my time on Sundays because of past experience. I'm sure you have something similar you can relate to from your past and chances are you're already pretty self-aware of it. So, keep doing everything you can to momage it in a way that makes things way better.

Being Present

One thing I've found to be a huge game changer, yet often need to still remind myself of, is living in the present. When you momage your time, you're often thinking ahead and reflecting behind. I've learned the hard way that going in either of these directions too frequently often doesn't lead you to the destination you were looking for. The GPS of life is going to reroute you so many times, frustrating the shit out of you, and sometimes making you want to give up altogether. You'll feel overwhelmed, resentful, regretful, and discouraged by it all. When you don't make a conscious effort to be present daily, you lose out on everything you're living for.

What do I mean by this?

Some days I feel like the only conversations I'm having with my kids are telling them what to do.

Brush your teeth.
Get dressed.
Make your bed.

Have you brushed your teeth?
Time to go, put your shoes on.
Don't touch that.
Tell your brother you're sorry.
Are your teeth brushed?
Clean up.
Share.
Did you flush the toilet?

When I take a minute to realize that every single thing I've said to my kids that day is a command, I remind myself to take a breather and to be grateful for them, for being their mom, for that moment with their sweet, high pitched kid voices that often say hysterical things or ask innocent and curious questions, and that I get to be there to actually listen to what they're saying. Living in the present often leads to being a more grateful person in general, which ultimately means you're living a more fulfilled and balanced life. Name one person who doesn't want that. I dare you.

Everyone has time to take a moment a day to be present. People usually have more than just a moment, actually. We're not used to that, though. Sometimes it even feels uncomfortable. We're used to go-go-go. We're used to filling those moments with social media or bitching about the past or meal planning for the week ahead. We're used to feeling guilty for taking a minute to breathe. Taking a minute to breathe isn't going to interrupt your plan or make you achieve your goals any less quickly. Taking a minute to breathe isn't going to take up any significant amount of time in your time momagement schedule. It is going to give you back the air you're lacking. It is going to bring pep back into your step and propel you further. It is going to remind you of why you wake up each day. It is going to turn your resting, tired bitch face into resting, still tired babe face.

People momage staying present in many different ways. They write a gratitude journal. They pray. They put their phones out of site (and hopefully out of mind) when they want to disconnect from work, social media, or any form of life outside their four walls and reconnect with their families. They ask their kids to play a game or read a book, rather than wait for their kids to ask them. They take the reality of a situation and make the best of it.

I've done all these things, and they've drastically changed how I momage my time and think about my days. Shifting your mindset to one of more gratitude makes you a generally happier person. When you're a happier person, you feel motivated to do great things. You feel satisfied with where you are even if you still have a laundry list of goals you want to achieve. You feel like even the shittiest situations bring you joy because you turn them around and make them work for you. Before you start thinking I'm a hippie on LSD tripping out right now, let me tell you what I mean here. I'm a realist, even more so than I'm an optimist. Maybe it's the native New Yorker, those cynical, geographical genetics, or just the practicality I was raised with. Nonetheless, I'm not trying to recruit you to my happy cult or drink my happy kool-aide. But perspective truly is the way to living a better life. It doesn't mean you lay down and die. It doesn't mean you are 100% satisfied with everything and everyone surrounding you. It does mean you choose to find the good in everyday rather than the shit in it. Wayne Dyer couldn't have spoken more truthful words when he said, "If you change the way you look at things, the things you look at change." It's literally that simple.

As a working mom, I commute on the regular. Four days per week, I take public transportation to San Francisco and then walk about half a mile to my office. It takes over an hour each way door to door. If I told you I loved it, you'd say I was lying, and I'd say, "You're absolutely right, girlfriend. Commuting sucks." The bottom line is though, commuting is part of my reality and maybe part of yours too. Commuting is a time suck, and commuting takes time away from other things I'd love to do with my time every day. Commuting also gives me the opportunity to listen to audiobooks, organize myself with to-do lists, online shop for essential things I'd likely be running to Target for, hear my favorite songs, power walk a mile a day, and sometimes even catch up with friends on a phone call. Commuting is a total bitch if you look at her with your bitch glasses on. Commuting is a total peach if you look at her with your rose-colored glasses on. Most days, I choose to see her in a shade of my favorite color: pink. Some days, I can't stand her, but I think that's a normal part of any relationship. I'm sure there are days even the people you love most in your life piss you off and make you angry. By the way, I won't take my relationship with commuting that far. I'd never say I *love* her. In the end, though, you either choose to see things for the good they bring you or the bad they leave you with—your choice.

Living a Mindful Life

A super small thing you can do to make a lasting impact on your gratitude scale is replacing the word 'have' with 'get.' Let's practice.

"I have to drop the kids off at school." Vs. "I get to drop the kids off at school."

"I have to go to that meeting." Vs. "I get to go to that meeting."

"I have to work out." Vs. "I get to work out."

In 2018, I was interviewed for something called the Mama Knows Best Summit. We talked about how making small changes to your day-to-day can lead to tremendous influence on your overall life. Remember when I told you to stop saying, "I don't have time" and start replacing it with, "It's not a priority to me." This is exactly what I'm talking about. It shifts your mindset.

When you replace 'have' with 'get,' your brain starts to process that action not as a required task, but as a sought-after action. When you see things differently, they feel different, and you feel different. Period.

"I have to drop the kids off at school," translates to "This is part of my day-to-day, and I need to get it done. Nothing fancy about that."

"I get to drop the kids off at school," translates to "My schedule allows me the flexibility and opportunity to do this for my littles."

"I have to go to that meeting," translates to "The content won't be interesting, and I could be doing something else if I didn't have to be there."

"I get to go to that meeting," translates to "My position allows me to be part of the discussion and contribute to the plans and outcome when it comes to that topic."

"I have to go to the gym," translates to "I need to work out because I'm too fat, not strong enough, or need to lose weight."

"I get to go to the gym," translates to "I'm excited to improve my body, get stronger, or look better."

See the difference? This is huge. This is motivating. This is highlighting things and opening your eyes to realizing that whatever you get to do is something you want to do rather than something you need or have to do. This is living a mindful life, and this is life-changing.

Let's Recap

- Obstacles, distractions, and past experience are not a reason to sidetrack you from your time momagement goals. Be in control—you're already pretty good at it.
- Figure out how to be present on the regular, even for a moment a day.
- Adopt an attitude of gratitude.
- Replace 'have' with 'get.' Change your mindset, change your life.

Chapter 9

Life Hacks

"If you want something you've never had, you've got to do something you've never done."
                    -Thomas Jefferson

In this chapter, you'll learn:

- My life hacks. Enjoy!

I bet you're thinking, "Shit-this B waited until the last chapter of her book to give me the quick and dirty version of how to momage my time and my life." Girl, you're damn right I did. You need to read *all of this* before you can get these tips because these aren't the answer to making major changes. These are helpful, yes. These are time-saving, yes. These are sanity delivering, hell yes. But the truth of the matter is, nothing changes if nothing changes. If you want change, you've got to make change. I hope that's sunken in thus far in this little number I've put together for you.

Nonetheless, sometimes you just need some practical, day-to-day tricks to manage the craziness of the life you're living. Your mom life, wife life, work life, fill-in-the-blank life can get the best of you, I know. So, here are my best tips for you not only to stay afloat but win the swim competition. I call these my *life hacks*.

Life Hack #1: Cook

If healthy eating is important to you (I hope it is) and meal time with your family is too, cook. Cooking every day is not smart, but eating homecooked meals (almost) every day is. I cook for the equivalent of a football team when I make something a little more complicated or time-consuming in my house. For example, I just may be the very best 'lasagna cooker,' as my kids call me, in the whole damn world. Lasagna in my house is no easy feat. I don't use jar sauce or shredded cheese. I use the real deal, good shit from scratch, baby. Making lasagna takes hours. It also makes my family and me really happy and allows some weeknight meals to be totally cooked with a simple oven pre-heat and 45 minutes of non-cooking kind of cooking. If you have a family fav or slightly complex dish, cook enough for at least three dinners when you make it. Then package it up nicely and store in your fridge or freezer for stress-free (and time free) meals.

Life Hack #2: Prep

Are you a sleep in kinda girl or a wake up early kinda girl? Let me clarify, ain't no mom technically sleeping in, but is it more important for you to have those extra few minutes to snooze in the AM or do you prefer to hit your bed uber early the night before and get up with the roosters? Personally, I like a good snooze (or two or three) in the morning. Consequently, I'd rather prep as much as possible the night before so I have the luxury of more time in the morning to sleep. What do I do? All of it. I pack diaper bags, lunch boxes, and my own stuff for work if I'm commuting the next day. I lay out my clothes and even choose accessories, so I don't have to make a lot of decisions in the morning. I make sure my kitchen's clean and my house is in (somewhat) order, so I don't wake up to chaos. These small steps, while some days are not easy, always make me feel more relaxed and able to start my next day on a positive note.

Life Hack # 3: Make-Up

Figure out a make-up routine that takes you 10 minutes or less. Honestly, mine can even take five minutes most days. Make-up is not something you should forgo. As women, we are so damn lucky to have this magical tool to make us look like we've actually slept eight hours or have high cheekbones. If you're no make-up guru, take your ass to a MAC counter (or your make-up brand of preference) and tell the sweet, make-up artist you need an everyday look that takes you 10 minutes or less and then let her make you over, mama. She will take more than 10 minutes because she will want to sell you more. That's ok. Enjoy the you-time. Also, take it as an opportunity to learn how and what to apply. Every time I do this, I learn a new tip. It's like getting free lessons, leaving beautiful and treating yourself to some new gifts. Win-win-win. Invest the short time it will take you to pop on some basic make-up every day, even if you're just momming that day. You will look and feel more put together, more beautiful, and more confident and be motivated to do so much more. Trust me.

Life Hack #4: Hair

Bad hair days are ok, but not every day should be one. How often do you wash your hair, really? I wash mine two to three times per week. I've gotten into the habit that every time I wash it, I do it. I don't know what kind of hair you have and what that means to you: blow dry, diffuse, curl, whatever, just do it. Your hair will look fabulous, last longer, and your bad hair days will be limited. Invest in some good hair products and some (write this down if you don't own it) dry shampoo. Dry shampoo will save you lots, I mean lots, of time without making you feel like you're having a bad hair day. Spend a little more on your hair products. The time and money you will spend to repair your hair at a salon won't be as necessary if you're using the right products in the meantime.

Life Hack #5: Home

Design your home in a functional and beautiful way. This doesn't mean you need a lot of money or a lot of space. Ikea has tons of inexpensive and simple products and furniture to do this. If that's not your style, there are so many websites with affordable options and free shipping to help you get there. Or, if you have the time luxury of strolling through a Homegoods, that's always a nice plus. What are your pain points in your house? Does your front door area get cluttered with shoes? Turn your entry table into a bench with storage and throw the shoes in there. A good friend of mine said she was always running up and down the stairs because her kids never had socks on when it was time to leave the house. She got a cute basket and filled it with socks by her door, next to the shoes. Makes a lot of sense, doesn't it? Toys don't need to be in every room of your home, and they don't need to be stored in kid-like, multicolored, ugly AF containers. Every piece of furniture in my house has closed storage, yet my house still feels super open, airy, and spacious. Utilize space that seems like it makes sense for your life, even if your house wasn't designed that way. We had completely unused space under our open staircase. We'd talked about closing it forever and making a storage closet. It was one of those projects that just never hit the priority list. I finally bought four hooks and a small piece of furniture and made it into an area where I could store kids' jackets, backpacks, and shoes and, most importantly, find everything we needed to get out the door on time for school.

Life Hack #6: Phone

Put your phone away in the evening hours. Ain't no one going to die on the group text or in social media land or on corporate email (unless someone really is, then please go for it) if you aren't contributing to the conversation. Many of them are pointless and not time sensitive. You'll be surprised how much this simple act can give you so many more minutes, mindful minutes at that, with the people that matter most to you. I leave my phone in my purse from the minute I walk in the door from my commute home until my kids are asleep. By doing this, I've been able to disconnect from work, social media, and any other distraction, keeping them all out of site and mind until I'm ready to look at them again later. My second shift, the mom shift, in the evening hours should get my undivided attention like my other work does. Also, without the distraction of a phone, I can get all my evening clean-up and chores done in less than half the time because I'm not distracted checking *just one thing*, that usually ends up becoming 27 things and taking more time than the entire list of tasks would have to begin with.

Life Hack #7: Lists

Make lists. Make all sorts of lists. If you know me by now, you know I love a good list. I have a Samsung phone (don't judge me iPhone users), so I use my S-notes app to make my lists. Honestly, this is no frills. It's basically the MS notepad of the cellphone, but sometimes even a simple pencil to paper is good enough for me.

Examples of lists I make:

A. The ever so popular generic To-Do list for the week
B. The meal-planning list
C. The grocery list to fulfill the meal-planning list
D. The fun things to do this weekend list
E. The people to buy Christmas gifts for list

F. The items I will buy for the people on the Christmas gift list

And the list of lists goes on. Whatever list you decide, just make your list, mama. Lists hold you accountable, keep you focused, and, most importantly, save you time. Yes, planning (and list making) takes time, time up until reading this book, you probably thought you didn't have. As you've done some work and hopefully had some lightbulb moments by now, I imagine you're thinking right now about the right time in your day to make your lists. By the way, lists take just a few minutes to make and will make you feel much less overwhelmed, help you easily strategize how to execute your tasks, save you money (meal-planning and grocery lists are good examples), and basically are a huge necessity if you are going to momage your time like a pro.

Life Hack #8: Friends

You literally do not have to be friends with people you don't like. Period. Start distancing yourself from people who you spend time with that don't give you anything worthwhile. I don't mean drop a friend going through a difficult time. I do mean drop a friend going through a miserable life. I know that sounds slightly harsh, but when you realize how much time you've gained from not listening to someone else complain or the negative effect that person has on you, you'll have a lot more time for you. You won't need to dig yourself out of a deep, demotivating hole you're stuck in because those you're surrounding yourself with won't be pulling you down there anymore. Unfollow people who don't bring you something positive or worthwhile on social media and start politely declining invitations from these people. Create some space between you and them. Eventually, the gap will be too large and inconvenient for them to keep reaching out. If you need to and you think it will help them, have an honest conversation with those people about why you're doing it. I've found, though, that typically these convos go in one ear and out the other. I know that I'm not going to change or even motivate people to change when they don't want to change. So, I don't waste my time and energy on these people or these efforts.

Life Hack #9: Technology/Schedule

Get a shared app or system to ensure your family (and caregiver) are all on the same page. We use the Cozi app (not an affiliate) and put our au pair's schedule and all of the kids' activities on it. The Cozi app is also color-coded, so you set who is affected by that particular event by color and name. I used to get daily texts from my hubs asking what time our au pair's schedule finished that day, so he could be home in time. It wasn't the most efficient use of either of our time. Now, he just checks the app. If our schedule changes slightly, the app notifies the affected parties. It has saved me countless hours in communication within my core tribe. Maybe this is a simple whiteboard in your kitchen? Whatever works. I think technology nowadays is the way to go when it comes to scheduling; however, at least in my life.

Life Hack #10: Me-time

Finally, and maybe most importantly, invest in some you-time. This may seem like the least vital when you look at your list of to-dos and think about all the people depending on you all the time, but it's way harder to keep a plant thriving when it's nearly dead. Do something nice for yourself every day. Yes, every damn day. This can be as extravagant as a visit to the spa (not typical in my life) or as a simple as treating yourself to a latte or even ten minutes alone in the bathroom. Sometimes, my me-time is spending an extra few minutes in a super-hot shower singing one of my favorite songs out loud, full volume, private-room karaoke style. Give your mind a rest and be prepared to be mind blown how much more swift, savvy, and strong you are able to be, simply because you positively rewarded yourself somehow. You do this with your kids, don't you? Why not do it for you?

Closing

"Being a mother is learning about strengths you didn't know you had and dealing with fears you didn't know existed."
-Linda Wooten

Motherhood is the scariest place you'll likely ever find yourself in. There are feelings of doubt and fear and happiness and stress and so much more, typically all happening in the same millisecond. You'll question your sanity frequently. You'll second guess your decisions daily. You'll lash out at the ones you love most more often than you'd like to admit. If you're well equipped, you'll also amaze yourself at how you do it. You'll indulge in the compliments strangers on the street give you when they see you gliding through life with kids, groceries, your dog, and a full mental load all in tow. Once in a while, you'll even take a deep, grateful breath because these are the days, no matter how challenging they may be, you never want to forget.

Motherhood is a sacrifice of the physical body for many and the mental brain for all. But, not all sacrifices need to result in a self-loathing, pity party. An entire religion called Christianity was based on the ultimate human sacrifice, and we're not all feeling bad for Jesus, are we? No! We're praising Him. Well, if we're Christian we are.

Momage your time because you love your kids. Momage your time because you love your hubs or partner. Momage your time because you love your career. Most importantly, momage your time because you love yourself. And without you, there's no mama, wife, successful businesswoman, entrepreneur, daughter, sister, friend, woman. Yes, I will say it. You, mama, are a special snowflake. Momage your time because despite all the snow you may or may not see fall this year, your snowflake needs to be there. Not falling, but rising above and making itself stand out because it's not going to hit the ground and melt. It's going to do pirouettes in the air and take its daughter to ballet and its son to soccer and then sit down and do something nice for itself.

What I've learned over the years is that some things come easy and most things don't. The easy things are usually not the ones we remember. The easy things are fleeting and give us a short lived high. While they're important, they're not what gives us real substance in life. They're nice-to-haves, not have-to-haves. The harder things can suck at the moment, but will ultimately teach you, lead you, and grow you. Without these hard things, there is little purpose, unclear direction, and superficiality. What's a superficial, lost life without purpose? Not one I nor you probably want to live.

Your dreams shouldn't scratch the surface just because you're a mom, a wife, a corporate attorney, a caretaker for your father, the PTA president, or any other role you have. Go deep. You can do this no matter what your circumstances are. Momaging your time will get you back the time you need to do the things you want. It won't happen overnight. Big dreams take time. But, what I know is this. When you want something, and I mean, really want something, if you momage your time right, you'll get it.

I'll leave you with this, mama. I'm an oxymoron of a person. I'm a realist and an optimist. I'm a lover and, yes, sometimes can be a fighter (don't cross me). I'm laid back (a little) and intense (a lot). On all accounts though, dreams don't work unless you do. So, get up, get out and get going because just like wiping your kid's butt, ain't no one going to do it but you. In the words of Tina Fey, "You go through big chunks of time where you're just thinking, 'This is impossible. Oh, this is impossible.' And then you just keep going and you sort of do the impossible." Now, go do the impossible, mama. You got this.

The Three Day Test

Sample:

Time	Activity	Change?	How?	Multitask?	How?
12:00 AM- 1:00 AM	Sleep	No		No	
1:00 AM- 2:00 AM	Sleep	No		No	
2:00 AM- 3:00 AM	Sleep	No		No	
3:00 AM- 4:00 AM	Sleep	No		No	

Time	Activity	Change?	How?	Multitask?	How?
4:00 AM- 5:00 AM	Sleep	No		No	
5:00 AM- 5:30 AM	Sleep	No		No	
5:30 AM- 6:00 AM	Sleep	Yes	Do something for me before everyone wakes up.	No	
6:00 AM- 6:30 AM	Snooze alarm until 6:20, wake up and start getting ready	Yes	Stop snoozing and just wake the eff up!	No	

Time Momagement

Time	Activity	Change?	How?	Multitask?	How?
6:30 AM- 7:00 AM	Get dressed, make-up, hair, while managing kids	No		No	Wish I didn't have to multitask this as is. Should I wake up sooner?
7:00 AM- 7:30 AM	Get lunch prepped for work, prep dinner for tonight	No		No	Already sort of multitasking this...
7:30 AM- 8:00 AM	Leave the house, start commute by car then train	No		Yes	Listen to podcast; read, listen to a book; organize my week or month
8:00 AM- 8:30 AM	Continue commute on train, then walk to work	No		Yes	Listen to podcast; read, listen to a book; organize my week or month

Time	Activity	Change?	How?	Multitask?	How?
8:30 AM- 9:00 AM	Arrive at the office; check e-mails & check-in with team	No		No	
9:00 AM- 9:30 AM	Work: E-mails; breakfast	No		No	
9:30 AM- 10:00 AM	Work: Finish project that is due today	No		No	
10:00 AM- 10:30 AM	Work: Meeting with boss	No		No	

Time Momagement

Time	Activity	Change?	How?	Multitask?	How?
10:30 AM- 11:00 AM	*Work: Meeting with boss*	*No*		*No*	
11:00 AM- 11:30 AM	*Work: Meeting with boss*	*No*		*No*	
11:30 AM- 12:00 PM	*Work: Presentation prep*	*No*		*No*	
12:00 PM- 12:30 PM	*Work: Check e-mails*	*Yes*	*Take a real break; e-mails will be there when I'm back*	*Yes*	*Take care of an errand, make a phone call or work out*

Time	Activity	Change?	How?	Multitask?	How?
12:30 PM- 1:00 PM	Work: Lunch while checking e-mails	Yes	Take a real break; e-mails will be there when I'm back	Yes	Take care of an errand, make a phone call or work out
1:00 PM- 1:30 PM	Work: Meeting with Marketing	No		No	
1:30 PM- 2:00 PM	Work: Meeting with sales	No		No	
2:00 PM- 2:30 PM	Work: Check e-mails; downtime	No		Yes	Check tomorrow's agenda and schedule and plan for next day

Time Momagement

Time	Activity	Change?	How?	Multitask?	How?
2:30 PM– 3:00 PM	Work: review and finish project due today	No		No	
3:00 PM– 3:30 PM	Work: meeting with consultant	No		No	
3:30 PM– 4:00 PM	Work: really finish project due today	No		No	
4:00 PM– 4:30 PM	Work: scheduled call with customer	No		No	

Time	Activity	Change?	How?	Multitask?	How?
4:30 PM- 5:00 PM	Work: check-emails; downtime	No		Yes	Make that dentist appointment for kids
5:00 PM- 5:30 PM	Leave work: walk to train, start commute	No		Yes	Call a friend or text / catch up with the girls
5:30 PM- 6:00 PM	Commute on train, then drive home	No		Yes	Decompress: meditate or listen to some good jams
6:00 PM- 6:30 PM	Get home; chat with kids; help with dinner	No		Yes	Cook while talking while refereeing three kids

Time Momagement

Time	Activity	Change?	How?	Multitask?	How?
6:30 PM- 7:00 PM	*Eat dinner together, then clean up*	*No*		*No*	
7:00 PM- 7:30 PM	*Bath time!*	*Yes*	*I could delegate this?*	*No*	
7:30 PM- 8:00 PM	*Toddler's bedtime routine*	*Yes*	*I could delegate this, but I don't want to*	*No*	
8:00 PM- 8:30 PM	*Twins' bedtime routine*	*Yes*	*I could delegate this, but I don't want to*	*No*	

Marisa Volpe Lonic

Time	Activity	Change?	How?	Multitask?	How?
8:30 PM- 9:00 PM	Social media rabbit hole (one thing turned into 25 minutes)	Yes	Don't check that one thing! Put phone out of site	Yes	Get Pinterest ideas for next week's meal plan
9:00 PM- 9:30 PM	Shower, prep for next day	Yes	I could shower in the am or later at night	Yes	Make easy decisions; prep as much as possible for next morning
9:30 PM- 10:00 PM	Check e-mail, then cruise social media again	Yes	Set a timer and only allow 10 minutes for this	Yes	Multi-task the mindless. Prep lunches while doing this
10:00 PM- 10:30 PM	Watch a show and fall asleep	Yes	Spend this time working on a Time Momage-ment goal	Yes	Multi-task the mindless. Fold some laundry while doing this

Time Momagement

Time	Activity	Change?	How?	Multitask?	How?
10:30 PM- 11:00 PM	Sleep	Yes	Spend this time working on a Time Momage- ment goal	No	
11:00 PM- 11:30 PM	Sleep	No		No	
11:30 PM- 12:00 AM	Sleep	No		No	

Sample Takeaways:

1. *I could easily use my commute to do something for me.*
2. *I didn't include the 30 times I "quickly" check social media throughout the day.*
3. *I love my sleep, but I could start my day off on a much better note if I had 15 minutes for coffee in peace before everyone wakes up.*

Time Momagement

Day 1:

Time	Activity	Change?	How?	Multitask?	How?
12:00 AM- 1:00 AM					
1:00 AM- 2:00 AM					
2:00 AM- 3:00 AM					
3:00 AM- 4:00 AM					

Time Momagement

Day 1:

Time	Activity	Change?	How?	Multitask?	How?
12:00 AM- 1:00 AM					
1:00 AM- 2:00 AM					
2:00 AM- 3:00 AM					
3:00 AM- 4:00 AM					

169

Time	Activity	Change?	How?	Multitask?	How?
4:00 AM- 5:00 AM					
5:00 AM- 5:30 AM					
5:30 AM- 6:00 AM					
6:00 AM- 6:30 AM					

Time Momagement

Time	Activity	Change?	How?	Multitask?	How?
6:30 AM- 7:00 AM					
7:00 AM- 7:30 AM					
7:30 AM- 8:00 AM					
8:00 AM- 8:30 AM					

Marisa Volpe Lonic

Time	Activity	Change?	How?	Multitask?	How?
8:30 AM- 9:00 AM					
9:00 AM- 9:30 AM					
9:30 AM- 10:00 AM					
10:00 AM- 10:30 AM					

Time Momagement

Time	Activity	Change?	How?	Multitask?	How?
10:30 AM- 11:00 AM					
11:00 AM- 11:30 AM					
11:30 AM- 12:00 PM					
12:00 PM- 12:30 PM					

Time	Activity	Change?	How?	Multitask?	How?
12:30 PM– 1:00 PM					
1:00 PM– 1:30 PM					
1:30 PM– 2:00 PM					
2:00 PM– 2:30 PM					

Time Momagement

Time	Activity	Change?	How?	Multitask?	How?
2:30 PM- 3:00 PM					
3:00 PM- 3:30 PM					
3:30 PM- 4:00 PM					
4:00 PM- 4:30 PM					

Time	Activity	Change?	How?	Multitask?	How?
4:30 PM- 5:00 PM					
5:00 PM- 5:30 PM					
5:30 PM- 6:00 PM					
6:00 PM- 6:30 PM					

Time Momagement

Time	Activity	Change?	How?	Multitask?	How?
6:30 PM- 7:00 PM					
7:00 PM- 7:30 PM					
7:30 PM- 8:00 PM					
8:00 PM- 8:30 PM					

Time	Activity	Change?	How?	Multitask?	How?
8:30 PM- 9:00 PM					
9:00 PM- 9:30 PM					
9:30 PM- 10:00 PM					
10:00 PM- 10:30 PM					

Time Momagement

Time	Activity	Change?	How?	Multitask?	How?
10:30 PM- 11:00 PM					
11:00 PM- 11:30 PM					
11:30 PM- 12:00 AM					

Day 1 Takeaways:

1.

2.

3.

Day 2:

Time	Activity	Change?	How?	Multitask?	How?
12:00 AM- 1:00 AM					
1:00 AM- 2:00 AM					
2:00 AM- 3:00 AM					
3:00 AM- 4:00 AM					

Time	Activity	Change?	How?	Multitask?	How?
4:00 AM- 5:00 AM					
5:00 AM- 5:30 AM					
5:30 AM- 6:00 AM					
6:00 AM- 6:30 AM					

Time Momagement

Time	Activity	Change?	How?	Multitask?	How?
6:30 AM- 7:00 AM					
7:00 AM- 7:30 AM					
7:30 AM- 8:00 AM					
8:00 AM- 8:30 AM					

Time	Activity	Change?	How?	Multitask?	How?
8:30 AM- 9:00 AM					
9:00 AM- 9:30 AM					
9:30 AM- 10:00 AM					
10:00 AM- 10:30 AM					

Time Momagement

Time	Activity	Change?	How?	Multitask?	How?
10:30 AM- 11:00 AM					
11:00 AM- 11:30 AM					
11:30 AM- 12:00 PM					
12:00 PM- 12:30 PM					

Marisa Volpe Lonic

Time	Activity	Change?	How?	Multitask?	How?
12:30 PM- 1:00 PM					
1:00 PM- 1:30 PM					
1:30 PM- 2:00 PM					
2:00 PM- 2:30 PM					

Time Momagement

Time	Activity	Change?	How?	Multitask?	How?
2:30 PM- 3:00 PM					
3:00 PM- 3:30 PM					
3:30 PM- 4:00 PM					
4:00 PM- 4:30 PM					

Marisa Volpe Lonic

Time	Activity	Change?	How?	Multitask?	How?
4:30 PM- 5:00 PM					
5:00 PM- 5:30 PM					
5:30 PM- 6:00 PM					
6:00 PM- 6:30 PM					

Time Momagement

Time	Activity	Change?	How?	Multitask?	How?
6:30 PM- 7:00 PM					
7:00 PM- 7:30 PM					
7:30 PM- 8:00 PM					
8:00 PM- 8:30 PM					

Marisa Volpe Lonic

Time	Activity	Change?	How?	Multitask?	How?
8:30 PM- 9:00 PM					
9:00 PM- 9:30 PM					
9:30 PM- 10:00 PM					
10:00 PM- 10:30 PM					

Time Momagement

Time	Activity	Change?	How?	Multitask?	How?
10:30 PM- 11:00 PM					
11:00 PM- 11:30 PM					
11:30 PM- 12:00 AM					

Day 2 Takeaways:

    1.

    2.

    3.

Day 3:

Time	Activity	Change?	How?	Multitask?	How?
12:00 AM- 1:00 AM					
1:00 AM- 2:00 AM					
2:00 AM- 3:00 AM					
3:00 AM- 4:00 AM					

Time	Activity	Change?	How?	Multitask?	How?
4:00 AM- 5:00 AM					
5:00 AM- 5:30 AM					
5:30 AM- 6:00 AM					
6:00 AM- 6:30 AM					

Time Momagement

Time	Activity	Change?	How?	Multitask?	How?
6:30 AM- 7:00 AM					
7:00 AM- 7:30 AM					
7:30 AM- 8:00 AM					
8:00 AM- 8:30 AM					

Marisa Volpe Lonic

Time	Activity	Change?	How?	Multitask?	How?
8:30 AM- 9:00 AM					
9:00 AM- 9:30 AM					
9:30 AM- 10:00 AM					
10:00 AM- 10:30 AM					

Time Momagement

Time	Activity	Change?	How?	Multitask?	How?
10:30 AM- 11:00 AM					
11:00 AM- 11:30 AM					
11:30 AM- 12:00 PM					
12:00 PM- 12:30 PM					

Marisa Volpe Lonic

Time	Activity	Change?	How?	Multitask?	How?
12:30 PM- 1:00 PM					
1:00 PM- 1:30 PM					
1:30 PM- 2:00 PM					
2:00 PM- 2:30 PM					

Time Momagement

Time	Activity	Change?	How?	Multitask?	How?
2:30 PM- 3:00 PM					
3:00 PM- 3:30 PM					
3:30 PM- 4:00 PM					
4:00 PM- 4:30 PM					

Time	Activity	Change?	How?	Multitask?	How?
4:30 PM- 5:00 PM					
5:00 PM- 5:30 PM					
5:30 PM- 6:00 PM					
6:00 PM- 6:30 PM					

Time Momagement

Time	Activity	Change?	How?	Multitask?	How?
6:30 PM- 7:00 PM					
7:00 PM- 7:30 PM					
7:30 PM- 8:00 PM					
8:00 PM- 8:30 PM					

Marisa Volpe Lonic

Time	Activity	Change?	How?	Multitask?	How?
8:30 PM- 9:00 PM					
9:00 PM- 9:30 PM					
9:30 PM- 10:00 PM					
10:00 PM- 10:30 PM					

Time Momagement

Time	Activity	Change?	How?	Multitask?	How?
10:30 PM- 11:00 PM					
11:00 PM- 11:30 PM					
11:30 PM- 12:00 AM					

Day 3 Takeaways:

1.

2.

3.

About the Author

Marisa Volpe Lonic is a working mom of four and the founder of Mama Work It. She's a NY native, CA resider, and former world traveler (pre-kids). She's a thirty-something woman with 6 years of mama experience, 10 years of accomplished wifing, and 13 years of workin' it-corporate style. When she's not kickin' it with the five men she shares her house with, you can find her writing, taking photos, running...ok, walking with a little bit of running, or cooking. She dreams big, works hard, and tries her damnedest to be grateful every day.

Made in the USA
San Bernardino, CA
15 February 2020